Alfred Tennyson

Tiresias

And Other Poems

Alfred Tennyson

Tiresias
And Other Poems

ISBN/EAN: 9783744712354

Printed in Europe, USA, Canada, Australia, Japan

Cover: Foto ©Thomas Meinert / pixelio.de

More available books at **www.hansebooks.com**

TIRESIAS

AND OTHER POEMS

BY

ALFRED
LORD TENNYSON

D.C.L. P.I.

London
MACMILLAN AND CO.
1885

TO MY GOOD FRIEND

ROBERT BROWNING,

WHOSE GENIUS AND GENIALITY

WILL BEST APPRECIATE WHAT MAY BE BEST,

AND MAKE MOST ALLOWANCE FOR WHAT MAY BE WORST,

THIS VOLUME

IS

AFFECTIONATELY DEDICATED.

CONTENTS.

CONTENTS.

TO E. FITZGERALD.

OLD FITZ, who from your suburb grange,

    Where once I tarried for a while,

Glance at the wheeling Orb of change,

    And greet it with a kindly smile ;

Whom yet I see as there you sit

    Beneath your sheltering garden-tree,

And watch your doves about you flit,

    And plant on shoulder, hand and knee,

Or on your head their rosy feet,

    As if they knew your diet spares

Whatever moved in that full sheet

    Let down to Peter at his prayers ;

B

Who live on milk and meal and grass;

   And once for ten long weeks I tried

Your table of Pythagoras,

   And seem'd at first 'a thing enskied'

(As Shakespeare has it) airy-light

   To float above the ways of men,

Then fell from that half-spiritual height

   Chill'd, till I tasted flesh again

One night when earth was winter-black,

   And all the heavens flash'd in frost;

And on me, half-asleep, came back

   That wholesome heat the blood had lost,

And set me climbing icy capes

   And glaciers, over which there roll'd

To meet me long-arm'd vines with grapes

   Of Eshcol hugeness; for the cold

Without, and warmth within me, wrought

To mould the dream; but none can say

That Lenten fare makes Lenten thought,

   Who reads your golden Eastern lay,

Than which I know no version done

   In English more divinely well;

A planet equal to the sun

   Which cast it, that large infidel

Your Omar; and your Omar drew

   Full-handed plaudits from our best

In modern letters, and from two,

   Old friends outvaluing all the rest,

Two voices heard on earth no more;

   But we old friends are still alive,

And I am nearing seventy-four,

   While you have touch'd at seventy-five,

And so I send a birthday line

   Of greeting; and my son, who dipt

In some forgotten book of mine

    With sallow scraps of manuscript,

And dating many a year ago,

    Has hit on this, which you will take

My Fitz, and welcome, as I know

    Less for its own than for the sake

Of one recalling gracious times,

    When, in our younger London days,

You found some merit in my rhymes,

    And I more pleasure in your praise.

TIRESIAS.

I WISH I were as in the years of old,

While yet the blessed daylight made itself

Ruddy thro' both the roofs of sight, and woke

These eyes, now dull, but then so keen to seek

The meanings ambush'd under all they saw,

The flight of birds, the flame of sacrifice,

What omens may foreshadow fate to man

And woman, and the secret of the Gods.

My son, the Gods, despite of human prayer,

Are slower to forgive than human kings.

The great God, Arês, burns in anger still

Against the guiltless heirs of him from Tyre,

Our Cadmus, out of whom thou art, who found

Beside the springs of Dircê, smote, and still'd

Thro' all its folds the multitudinous beast,

The dragon, which our trembling fathers call'd

The God's own son.

               A tale, that told to me,

When but thine age, by age as winter-white

As mine is now, amazed, but made me yearn

For larger glimpses of that more than man

Which rolls the heavens, and lifts, and lays the deep,

Yet loves and hates with mortal hates and loves,

And moves unseen among the ways of men.

  Then, in my wanderings all the lands that lie

Subjected to the Heliconian ridge

Have heard this footstep fall, altho' my wont

Was more to scale the highest of the heights

With some strange hope to see the nearer God.

One naked peak—the sister of the sun

Would climb from out the dark, and linger there

To silver all the valleys with her shafts—

There once, but long ago, five-fold thy term

Of years, I lay; the winds were dead for heat;

The noonday crag made the hand burn; and sick

For shadow—not one bush was near—I rose

Following a torrent till its myriad falls

Found silence in the hollows underneath.

There in a secret olive-glade I saw

Pallas Athene climbing from the bath

In anger; yet one glittering foot disturb'd

The lucid well; one snowy knee was prest

Against the margin flowers; a dreadful light

Came from her golden hair, her golden helm

And all her golden armour on the grass,

And from her virgin breast, and virgin eyes

Remaining fixt on mine, till mine grew dark

For ever, and I heard a voice that said

' Henceforth be blind, for thou hast seen too much,

And speak the truth that no man may believe.'

　Son, in the hidden world of sight, that lives

Behind this darkness, I behold her still,

Beyond all work of those who carve the stone,

Beyond all dreams of Godlike womanhood,

Ineffable beauty, out of whom, at a glance,

And as it were, perforce, upon me flash'd

The power of prophesying—but to me

No power—so chain'd and coupled with the curse

Of blindness and their unbelief, who heard

And heard not, when I spake of famine, plague,

Shrine-shattering earthquake, fire, flood, thunder-

　　　bolt,

And angers of the Gods for evil done

And expiation lack'd—no power on Fate,

Theirs, or mine own ! for when the crowd would roar

For blood, for war, whose issue was their doom,

To cast wise words among the multitude

Was flinging fruit to lions ; nor, in hours

Of civil outbreak, when I knew the twain

Would each waste each, and bring on both the yoke

Of stronger states, was mine the voice to curb

The madness of our cities and their kings.

   Who ever turn'd upon his heel to hear

My warning that the tyranny of one

Was prelude to the tyranny of all ?

My counsel that the tyranny of all

Led backward to the tyranny of one ?

    This power hath work'd no good to aught that

      lives,

And these blind hands were useless in their wars.

O therefore that the unfulfill'd desire,

The grief for ever born from griefs to be,

The boundless yearning of the Prophet's heart—

Could *that* stand forth, and like a statue, rear'd

To some great citizen, win all praise from all

Who past it, saying, 'That was he!'

                              In vain!

Virtue must shape itself in deed, and those

Whom weakness or necessity have cramp'd

Within themselves, immerging, each, his urn

In his own well, draw solace as he may.

    Menaceus, thou hast eyes, and I can hear

Too plainly what full tides of onset sap

Our seven high gates, and what a weight of war

Rides on those ringing axles! jingle of bits,

Shouts, arrows, tramp of the hornfooted horse

That grind the glebe to powder! Stony showers

Of that ear-stunning hail of Arês crash

Along the sounding walls. Above, below,

Shock after shock, the song-built towers and gates

Reel, bruised and butted with the shuddering

War-thunder of iron rams ; and from within

The city comes a murmur void of joy,

Lest she be taken captive—maidens, wives,

And mothers with their babblers of the dawn,

And oldest age in shadow from the night,

Falling about their shrines before their Gods,

And wailing 'Save us.'

                   And they wail to thee !

These eyeless eyes, that cannot see thine own,

See this, that only in thy virtue lies

The saving of our Thebes ; for, yesternight,

To me, the great God Arês, whose one bliss

Is war, and human sacrifice—himself

Blood-red from battle, spear and helmet tipt

With stormy light as on a mast at sea,

Stood out before a darkness, crying 'Thebes,

Thy Thebes shall fall and perish, for I loathe

The seed of Cadmus—yet if one of these

By his own hand—if one of these———'

                                   My son,

No sound is breathed so potent to coerce,

And to conciliate, as their names who dare

For that sweet mother land which gave them birth

Nobly to do, nobly to die.   Their names,

Graven on memorial columns, are a song

Heard in the future; few, but more than wall

And rampart, their examples reach a hand

Far thro' all years, and everywhere they meet

And kindle generous purpose, and the strength

To mould it into action pure as theirs.

Fairer thy fate than mine, if life's best end

Be to end well! and thou refusing this,

Unvenerable will thy memory be

While men shall move the lips : but if thou dare—

Thou, one of these, the race of Cadmus—then

No stone is fitted in yon marble girth

Whose echo shall not tongue thy glorious doom,

Nor in this pavement but shall ring thy name

To every hoof that clangs it, and the springs

Of Dircê laving yonder battle-plain,

Heard from the roofs by night, will murmur thee

To thine own Thebes, while Thebes thro' thee shall stand

Firm-based with all her Gods.

                  The Dragon's cave

Half hid, they tell me, now in flowing vines—

Where once he dwelt and whence he roll'd himself

At dead of night—thou knowest, and that smooth

    rock

Before it, altar-fashion'd, where of late

The woman-breasted Sphinx, with wings drawn

    back,

Folded her lion paws, and look'd to Thebes.

There blanch the bones of whom she slew, and these

Mixt with her own, because the fierce beast found

A wiser than herself, and dash'd herself

Dead in her rage : but thou art wise enough,

Tho' young, to love thy wiser, blunt the curse

Of Pallas, hear, and tho' I speak the truth

Believe I speak it, let thine own hand strike

Thy youthful pulses into rest and quench

The red God's anger, fearing not to plunge

Thy torch of life in darkness, rather—thou

Rejoicing that the sun, the moon, the stars

Send no such light upon the ways of men

As one great deed.

               Thither, my son, and there

Thou, that hast never known the embrace of love,

Offer thy maiden life.

                 This useless hand !

I felt one warm tear fall upon it.   Gone !

He will achieve his greatness.

                   But for me,

I would that I were gather'd to my rest,

And mingled with the famous kings of old,

On whom about their ocean-islands flash

The faces of the Gods—the wise man's word,

Here trampled by the populace underfoot,

There crown'd with worship—and these eyes will find

The men I knew, and watch the chariot whirl

About the goal again, and hunters race

The shadowy lion, and the warrior-kings,

In height and prowess more than human, strive

Again for glory, while the golden lyre

Is ever sounding in heroic ears

Heroic hymns, and every way the vales

Wind, clouded with the grateful incense-fume

Of those who mix all odour to the Gods

On one far height in one far-shining fire.

———

'ONE height and one far-shining fire'

   And while I fancied that my friend

For this brief idyll would require

   A less diffuse and opulent end,

And would defend his judgment well,

   If I should deem it over nice—

The tolling of his funeral bell

Broke on my Pagan Paradise,

And mixt the dream of classic times,

And all the phantoms of the dream,

With present grief, and made the rhymes,

That miss'd his living welcome, seem

Like would-be guests an hour too late,

Who down the highway moving on

With easy laughter find the gate

Is bolted, and the master gone.

Gone into darkness, that full light

Of friendship! past, in sleep, away

By night, into the deeper night!

The deeper night? A clearer day

Than our poor twilight dawn on earth—

If night, what barren toil to be!

What life, so maim'd by night, were worth

Our living out? Not mine to me

C

Remembering all the golden hours

   Now silent, and so many dead,

And him the last; and laying flowers,

   This wreath, above his honour'd head,

And praying that, when I from hence

   Shall fade with him into the unknown,

My close of earth's experience

   May prove as peaceful as his own.

THE WRECK.

I.

HIDE me, Mother! my Fathers belong'd to the
church of old,

I am driven by storm and sin and death to the
ancient fold,

I cling to the Catholic Cross once more, to the
Faith that saves,

My brain is full of the crash of wrecks, and the
roar of waves,

My life itself is a wreck, I have sullied a noble
name,

I am flung from the rushing tide of the world as a
waif of shame,

I am roused by the wail of a child, and awake to a

    livid light,

And a ghastlier face than ever has haunted a grave

    by night,

I would hide from the storm without, I would flee

    from the storm within,

I would make my life one prayer for a soul that

    died in his sin,

I was the tempter, Mother, and mine was the

    deeper fall ;

I will sit at your feet, I will hide my face, I will

    tell you all.

II.

He that they gave me to, Mother, a heedless and

    innocent bride—

I never have wrong'd his heart, I have only wounded

    his pride—

Spain in his blood and the Jew——dark-visaged,
    stately and tall—

A princelier-looking man never stept thro' a Prince's
    hall.

And who, when his anger was kindled, would ven-
    ture to give him the nay?

And a man men fear is a man to be loved by the
    women they say.

And I could have loved him too, if the blossom
    can doat on the blight,

Or the young green leaf rejoice in the frost that
    sears it at night;

He would open the books that I prized, and toss
    them away with a yawn,

Repell'd by the magnet of Art to the which my
    nature was drawn,

The word of the Poet by whom the deeps of the
    world are stirr'd,

The music that robes it in language beneath and
    beyond the word !

My Shelley would fall from my hands when he cast
    a contemptuous glance

From where he was poring over his Tables of Trade
    and Finance ;

My hands, when I heard him coming would drop
    from the chords or the keys,

But ever I fail'd to please him, however I strove
    to please—

All day long far-off in the cloud of the city, and
    there

Lost, head and heart, in the chances of dividend,
    consol, and share—

And at home if I sought for a kindly caress, being
    woman and weak,

His formal kiss fell chill as a flake of snow on the
    cheek :

And so, when I bore him a girl, when I held it

    aloft in my joy,

He look'd at it coldly, and said to me 'Pity it isn't

    a boy.'

The one thing given me, to love and to live for,

    glanced at in scorn !

The child that I felt I could die for—as if she were

    basely born !

I had lived a wild-flower life, I was planted now in

    a tomb ;

The daisy will shut to the shadow, I closed my

    heart to the gloom ;

I threw myself all abroad—I would play my part

    with the young

By the low foot-lights of the world—and I caught

    the wreath that was flung.

III.

Mother, I have not—however their tongues may
  have babbled of me—

Sinn'd thro' an animal vileness, for all but a dwarf
  was he,

And all but a hunchback too; and I look'd at him,
  first, askance

With pity—not he the knight for an amorous girl's
  romance !

Tho' wealthy enough to have bask'd in the light of
  a dowerless smile,

Having lands at home and abroad in a rich West-
  Indian isle ;

But I came on him once at a ball, the heart of a
  listening crowd—

Why, what a brow was there ! he was seated—
  speaking aloud

To women, the flower of the time, and men at the

    helm of state—

Flowing with easy greatness and touching on all

    things great,

Science, philosophy, song—till I felt myself ready

    to weep

For I knew not what, when I heard that voice,—as

    mellow and deep

As a psalm by a mighty master and peal'd from an

    organ,—roll

Rising and falling—for, Mother, the voice was the

    voice of the soul ;

And the sun of the soul made day in the dark of

    his wonderful eyes.

Here was the hand that would help me, would heal

    me—the heart that was wise !

And he, poor man, when he learnt that I hated the

    ring I wore,

He helpt me with death, and he heal'd me with
sorrow for evermore.

IV.

For I broke the bond.   That day my nurse had
brought me the child.

The small sweet face was flush'd, but it coo'd to
the Mother and smiled.

'Anything ailing,' I ask'd her, 'with baby?'   She
shook her head,

And the Motherless Mother kiss'd it, and turn'd in
her haste and fled.

V.

Low warm winds had gently breathed us away from
the land—

Ten long sweet summer days upon deck, sitting
hand in hand—

When he clothed a naked mind with the wisdom
and wealth of his own,

And I bow'd myself down as a slave to his intel-
lectual throne,

When he coin'd into English gold some treasure of
classical song,

When he flouted a statesman's error, or flamed at
a public wrong,

When he rose as it were on the wings of an eagle
beyond me, and past

Over the range and the change of the world from
the first to the last,

When he spoke of his tropical home in the canes
by the purple tide,

And the high star-crowns of his palms on the deep-
wooded mountain-side,

And cliffs all robed in lianas that dropt to the brink
of his bay,

And trees like the towers of a minster, the sons of
a winterless day.

'Paradise there!' so he said, but I seem'd in Paradise then

With the first great love I had felt for the first and
greatest of men,

Ten long days of summer and sin—if it must be
so—

But days of a larger light than I ever again shall
know—

Days that will glimmer, I fear, thro' life to my latest
breath;

'No frost there,' so he said, 'as in truest Love no
Death.'

VI.

Mother, one morning a bird with a warble plain-
tively sweet

Perch'd on the shrouds, and then fell fluttering

   down at my feet ;

I took it, he made it a cage, we fondled it, Stephen

   and I,

But it died, and I thought of the child for a

   moment, I scarce know why.

VII.

But if sin be sin, not inherited fate, as many will

   say,

My sin to my desolate little one found me at sea

   on a day,

When her orphan wail came borne in the shriek of

   a growing wind,

And a voice rang out in the thunders of Ocean and

   Heaven 'Thou hast sinn'd.'

And down in the cabin were we, for the towering

   crest of the tides

Plunged on the vessel and swept in a cataract off

    from her sides,

And ever the great storm grew with a howl and a

    hoot of the blast

In the rigging, voices of hell—then came the crash

    of the mast.

'The wages of sin is death,' and then I began to

    weep,

'I am the Jonah, the crew should cast me into the

    deep,

For ah God, what a heart was mine to forsake her

    even for you.'

'Never the heart among women,' he said, 'more

    tender and true.'

'The heart! not a mother's heart, when I left my

    darling alone.'

'Comfort yourself, for the heart of the father will

    care for his own.'

'The heart of the father will spurn her,' I cried, 'for

    the sin of the wife,

The cloud of the mother's shame will enfold her

    and darken her life.'

Then his pale face twitch'd; 'O Stephen, I love

    you, I love you, and yet '—

As I lean'd away from his arms—'would God, we

    had never met !'

And he spoke not—only the storm ; till after a

    little, I yearn'd

For his voice again, and he call'd to me 'Kiss me !'

    and there—as I turn'd—

'The heart, the heart !' I kiss'd him, I clung to the

    sinking form,

And the storm went roaring above us, and he—

    was out of the storm.

VIII.

And then, then, Mother, the ship stagger'd under
a thunderous shock,

That shook us asunder, as if she had struck and
crash'd on a rock ;

For a huge sea smote every soul from the decks of
The Falcon but one ;

All of them, all but the man that was lash'd to the
helm had gone ;

And I fell—and the storm and the days went by,
but I knew no more—

Lost myself—lay like the dead by the dead on the
cabin floor,

Dead to the death beside me, and lost to the loss
that was mine,

With a dim dream, now and then, of a hand giving
bread and wine,

Till I woke from the trance, and the ship stood

    still, and the skies were blue,

But the face I had known, O Mother, was not the

    face that I knew.

IX.

The strange misfeaturing mask that I saw so amazed

    me, that I

Stumbled on deck, half mad. I would fling myself

    over and die !

But one—he was waving a flag—the one man left

    on the wreck—

'Woman'—he graspt at my arm—'stay there '—I

    crouch'd on the deck—

'We are sinking, and yet there's hope: look yonder,'

    he cried, 'a sail'

In a tone so rough that I broke into passionate

    tears, and the wail

Of a beaten babe, till I saw that a boat was nearing
  us—then

All on a sudden I thought, I shall look on the
  child again.

X.

They lower'd me down the side, and there in the
  boat I lay

With sad eyes fixt on the lost sea-home, as we
  glided away,

And I sigh'd, as the low dark hull dipt under the
  smiling main,

'Had I stay'd with *him*, I had now—with *him*—
  been out of my pain.'

XI.

They took us aboard: the crew were gentle, the
  captain kind;

But *I* was the lonely slave of an often-wandering
  mind;

For whenever a rougher gust might tumble a

    stormier wave,

'O Stephen,' I moan'd, 'I am coming to thee in

    thine Ocean-grave.'

And again, when a balmier breeze curl'd over a

    peacefuller sea,

I found myself moaning again 'O child, I am

    coming to thee.'

XII.

The broad white brow of the Isle—that bay with

    the colour'd sand—

Rich was the rose of sunset there, as we drew to

    the land;

All so quiet the ripple would hardly blanch into

    spray

At the feet of the cliff; and I pray'd—'my child'

    —for I still could pray—

'May her life be as blissfully calm, be never
  gloom'd by the curse

Of a sin, not hers!'

                    Was it well with the child?

                              I wrote to the nurse

Who had borne my flower on her hireling heart;
  and an answer came

Not from the nurse—nor yet to the wife—to her
  maiden name!

I shook as I open'd the letter—I knew that hand
  too well—

And from it a scrap, clipt out of the 'deaths' in a
  paper, fell.

'Ten long sweet summer days' of fever, and want
  of care!

And gone—that day of the storm—O Mother, she
  came to me there

DESPAIR.

A man and his wife having lost faith in a God, and hope of a life to come, and being utterly miserable in this, resolve to end themselves by drowning. The woman is drowned, but the man rescued by a minister of the sect he had abandoned.

I.

Is it you, that preach'd in the chapel there looking

over the sand?

Follow'd us too that night, and dogg'd us, and drew

me to land?

II.

What did I feel that night? You are curious.

How should I tell?

Does it matter so much what I felt? You rescued
    me—yet—was it well

That you came unwish'd for, uncall'd, between me
    and the deep and my doom,

Three days since, three more dark days of the
    Godless gloom

Of a life without sun, without health, without hope,
    without any delight

In anything here upon earth? but ah God, that
    night, that night

When the rolling eyes of the light-house there on
    the fatal neck

Of land running out into rock—they had saved
    many hundreds from wreck—

Glared on our way toward death, I remember I
    thought, as we past,

Does it matter how many they saved? we are all
    of us wreck'd at last—

'Do you fear,' and there came thro' the roar of the

breaker a whisper, a breath,

'Fear? am I not with you? I am frighted at life

not death.'

III.

And the suns of the limitless Universe sparkled

and shone in the sky,

Flashing with fires as of God, but we knew that

their light was a lie—

Bright as with deathless hope—but, however they

sparkled and shone,

The dark little worlds running round them were

worlds of woe like our own—

No soul in the heaven above, no soul on the earth

below,

A fiery scroll written over with lamentation and

woe.

IV.

See, we were nursed in the drear night-fold of your
fatalist creed,

And we turn'd to the growing dawn, we had hoped
for a dawn indeed,

When the light of a Sun that was coming would
scatter the ghosts of the Past,

And the cramping creeds that had madden'd the
peoples would vanish at last,

And we broke away from the Christ, our human
brother and friend,

For He spoke, or it seem'd that He spoke, of a
Hell without help, without end.

V.

Hoped for a dawn and it came, but the promise
had faded away;

We had past from a cheerless night to the glare of

    a drearier day ;

He is only a cloud and a smoke who was once a

    pillar of fire,

The guess of a worm in the dust and the shadow

    of its desire—

Of a worm as it writhes in a world of the weak

    trodden down by the strong,

Of a dying worm in a world, all massacre, murder,

    and wrong.

VI.

O we poor orphans of nothing—alone on that lonely

    shore—

Born of the brainless Nature who knew not that

    which she bore !

Trusting no longer that earthly flower would be

    heavenly fruit—

Come from the brute, poor souls—no souls—and
to die with the brute——

VII.

Nay, but I am not claiming your pity : I know you
of old—

Small pity for those that have ranged from the
narrow warmth of your fold,

Where you bawl'd the dark side of your faith and a
God of eternal rage,

Till you flung us back on ourselves, and the human
heart, and the Age.

VIII.

But pity—the Pagan held it a vice—was in her and
in me,

Helpless, taking the place of the pitying God that
should be !

Pity for all that aches in the grasp of an idiot
power,

And pity for our own selves on an earth that bore
not a flower;

Pity for all that suffers on land or in air or the deep,

And pity for our own selves till we long'd for eternal
sleep.

IX.

' Lightly step over the sands ! the waters—you hear
them call !

Life with its anguish, and horrors, and errors—away
with it all !'

And she laid her hand in my own—she was always
loyal and sweet—

Till the points of the foam in the dusk came playing
about our feet.

There was a strong sea-current would sweep us out
to the main.

'Ah God' tho' I felt as I spoke I was taking the
name in vain—

'Ah God' and we turn'd to each other, we kiss'd,
we embraced, she and I,

Knowing the Love we were used to believe everlasting would die :

We had read their know-nothing books and we lean'd
to the darker side—

Ah God, should we find Him, perhaps, perhaps, if
we died, if we died ;

We never had found Him on earth, this earth is a
fatherless Hell—

'Dear Love, for ever and ever, for ever and ever
farewell,'

Never a cry so desolate, not since the world began,

Never a kiss so sad, no, not since the coming of
man !

X.

But the blind wave cast me ashore, and you saved
me, a valueless life.

Not a grain of gratitude mine ! You have parted
the man from the wife.

I am left alone on the land, she is all alone in the
sea ;

If a curse meant ought, I would curse you for not
having let me be.

XI.

Visions of youth—for my brain was drunk with the
water, it seems ;

I had past into perfect quiet at length out of
pleasant dreams,

And the transient trouble of drowning—what was

　　it when match'd with the pains

Of the hellish heat of a wretched life rushing back

　　thro' the veins?

XII.

Why should I live? one son had forged on his

　　father and fled,

And if I believed in a God, I would thank him,

　　the other is dead,

And there was a baby-girl, that had never look'd

　　on the light:

Happiest she of us all, for she past from the night

　　to the night.

XIII.

But the crime, if a crime, of her eldest-born, her

　　glory, her boast,

Struck hard at the tender heart of the mother, and

    broke it almost ;

Tho', glory and shame dying out for ever in endless

    time,

Does it matter so much whether crown'd for a virtue,

    or hang'd for a crime?

XIV.

And ruin'd by *him*, by *him*, I stood there, naked,

    amazed

In a world of arrogant opulence, fear'd myself

    turning crazed,

And I would not be mock'd in a madhouse ! and

    she, the delicate wife,

With a grief that could only be cured, if cured, by

    the surgeon's knife,—

XV.

Why should we bear with an hour of torture, a
moment of pain,

If every man die for ever, if all his griefs are in vain,

And the homeless planet at length will be wheel'd

thro' the silence of space,

Motherless evermore of an ever-vanishing race,

When the worm shall have writhed its last, and its

last brother-worm will have fled

From the dead fossil skull that is left in the rocks

of an earth that is dead?

XVI.

Have I crazed myself over their horrible infidel

writings? O yes,

For these are the new dark ages, you see, of the

popular press,

When the bat comes out of his cave, and the owls

    are whooping at noon,

And Doubt is the lord of this dunghill and crows

    to the sun and the moon,

Till the Sun and the Moon of our science are both

    of them turn'd into blood,

And Hope will have broken her heart, running

    after a shadow of good;

For their knowing and know-nothing books are

    scatter'd from hand to hand—

We have knelt in your know-all chapel too looking

    over the sand.

XVII.

What! I should call on that Infinite Love that has

    served us so well?

Infinite cruelty rather that made everlasting Hell,

E

Made us, foreknew us, foredoom'd us, and does
what he will with his own ;

Better our dead brute mother who never has heard
us groan !

XVIII.

Hell? if the souls of men were immortal, as men
have been told,

The lecher would cleave to his lusts, and the miser
would yearn for his gold,

And so there were Hell for ever ! but were there a
God as you say,

His Love would have power over Hell till it utterly
vanish'd away.

XIX.

Ah yet—I have had some glimmer, at times, in
my gloomiest woe,

Of a God behind all—after all—the great God for

    aught that I know;

But the God of Love and of Hell together—they

    cannot be thought,

If there be such a God, may the Great God curse

    him and bring him to nought!

XX.

Blasphemy! whose is the fault? is it mine? for

    why would you save

A madman to vex you with wretched words, who

    is best in his grave?

Blasphemy! ay, why not, being damn'd beyond

    hope of grace?

O would I were yonder with her, and away from

    your faith and your face!

Blasphemy ! true ! I have scared you pale with my

    scandalous talk,

But the blasphemy to *my* mind lies all in the way

    that you walk.

XXI.

Hence ! she is gone ! can I stay ? can I breathe

    divorced from the Past ?

You needs must have good lynx-eyes if I do not

    escape you at last.

Our orthodox coroner doubtless will find it a felo-

    de-se,

And the stake and the cross-road, fool, if you will,

    does it matter to me ?

THE ANCIENT SAGE.

A THOUSAND summers ere the time of Christ

From out his ancient city came a Seer

Whom one that loved, and honour'd him, and yet

Was no disciple, richly garb'd, but worn

From wasteful living, follow'd—in his hand

A scroll of verse—till that old man before

A cavern whence an affluent fountain pour'd

From darkness into daylight, turn'd and spoke.

This wealth of waters might but seem to draw

From yon dark cave, but, son, the source is higher,

Yon summit half-a-league in air—and higher,

The cloud that hides it—higher still, the heavens

Whereby the cloud was moulded, and whereout

The cloud descended.   Force is from the heights.

I am wearied of our city, son, and go

To spend my one last year among the hills.

What hast thou there?   Some deathsong for the
        Ghouls

To make their banquet relish? let me read.

        " How far thro' all the bloom and brake

            That nightingale is heard !

        What power but the bird's could make

            This music in the bird?

        How summer-bright are yonder skies,

            And earth as fair in hue !

        And yet what sign of aught that lies

            Behind the green and blue?

But man to-day is fancy's fool
As man hath ever been.
The nameless Power, or Powers, that rule
Were never heard or seen."

If thou would'st hear the Nameless, and wilt dive

Into the Temple-cave of thine own self,

There, brooding by the central altar, thou

May'st haply learn the Nameless hath a voice,

By which thou wilt abide, if thou be wise,

As if thou knewest, tho' thou canst not know;

For Knowledge is the swallow on the lake

That sees and stirs the surface-shadow there

But never yet hath dipt into the abysm,

The Abysm of all Abysms, beneath, within

The blue of sky and sea, the green of earth,

And in the million-millionth of a grain

Which cleft and cleft again for evermore,

And ever vanishing, never vanishes,

To me, my son, more mystic than myself,

Or even than the Nameless is to me.

　　And when thou sendest thy free soul thro' heaven,

Nor understandest bound nor boundlessness,

Thou seest the Nameless of the hundred names.

　　And if the Nameless should withdraw from all

Thy frailty counts most real, all thy world

Might vanish like thy shadow in the dark.

　　" And since—from when this earth began—

　　　　The Nameless never came

　　Among us, never spake with man,

　　　　And never named the Name "—

Thou canst not prove the Nameless, O my son,

Nor canst thou prove the world thou movest in,

Thou canst not prove that thou art body alone,

Nor canst thou prove that thou art spirit alone

Nor canst thou prove that thou art both in one :

Thou canst not prove thou art immortal, no

Nor yet that thou art mortal—nay my son,

Thou canst not prove that I, who speak with
    thee,

Am not thyself in converse with thyself,

For nothing worthy proving can be proven,

Nor yet disproven : wherefore thou be wise,

Cleave ever to the sunnier side of doubt,

And cling to Faith beyond the forms of Faith !

She reels not in the storm of warring words,

She brightens at the clash of ' Yes ' and ' No,'

She sees the Best that glimmers thro' the Worst,

She feels the Sun is hid but for a night,

She spies the summer thro' the winter bud,

She tastes the fruit before the blossom falls,

She hears the lark within the songless egg,

She finds the fountain where they wail'd ' Mirage ' !

　　" What Power? aught akin to Mind,

　　　　The mind in me and you ?

　　Or power as of the Gods gone blind

　　　　Who see not what they do?"

But some in yonder city hold, my son,

That none but Gods could build this house of ours,

So beautiful, vast, various, so beyond

All work of man, yet, like all work of man,

A beauty with defect——till That which knows,

And is not known, but felt thro' what we feel

Within ourselves is highest, shall descend

On this half-deed, and shape it at the last

According to the Highest in the Highest.

"What Power but the Years that make

    And break the vase of clay,

And stir the sleeping earth, and wake

    The bloom that fades away?

What rulers but the Days and Hours

    That cancel weal with woe,

And wind the front of youth with flowers,

    And cap our age with snow?"

The days and hours are ever glancing by,

And seem to flicker past thro' sun and shade,

Or short, or long, as Pleasure leads, or Pain;

But with the Nameless is nor Day nor Hour;

Tho' we, thin minds, who creep from thought to

    thought

Break into 'Thens' and 'Whens' the Eternal Now:

This double seeming of the single world!—

My words are like the babblings in a dream

Of nightmare, when the babblings break the dream.

But thou be wise in this dream-world of ours,

Nor take thy dial for thy deity,

But make the passing shadow serve thy will.

          " The years that made the stripling wise

              Undo their work again,

          And leave him, blind of heart and eyes,

              The last and least of men ;

          Who clings to earth, and once would dare

              Hell-heat or Arctic cold,

          And now one breath of cooler air

              Would loose him from his hold ;

          His winter chills him to the root,

              He withers marrow and mind ;

          The kernel of the shrivell'd fruit

Is jutting thro' the rind ;

The tiger spasms tear his chest,

The palsy wags his head ;

The wife, the sons, who love him best

Would fain that he were dead ;

The griefs by which he once was wrung

Were never worth the while "—

Who knows ? or whether this earth-narrow life

Be yet but yolk, and forming in the shell ?

" The shaft of scorn that once had stung

But wakes a dotard smile."

The placid gleam of sunset after storm !

" The statesman's brain that sway'd the past

Is feebler than his knees ;

The passive sailor wrecks at last

In ever-silent seas ;

The warrior hath forgot his arms,

The Learned all his lore ;

The changing market frets or charms

The merchant's hope no more ;

The prophet's beacon burn'd in vain,

And now is lost in cloud ;

The plowman passes, bent with pain,

To mix with what he plow'd ;

The poet whom his Age would quote

As heir of endless fame—

He knows not ev'n the book he wrote,

Not even his own name.

For man has overlived his day,

And, darkening in the light,

Scarce feels the senses break away

To mix with ancient Night."

The shell must break before the bird can fly.

" The years that when my Youth began

    Had set the lily and rose

By all my ways where'er they ran,

    Have ended mortal foes ;

My rose of love for ever gone,

    My lily of truth and trust—

They made her lily and rose in one,

    And changed her into dust.

O rosetree planted in my grief,

    And growing, on her tomb,

Her dust is greening in your leaf,

    Her blood is in your bloom.

O slender lily waving there,

    And laughing back the light,

In vain you tell me ' Earth is fair '

    When all is dark as night."

My son, the world is dark with griefs and graves,

So dark that men cry out against the Heavens.

Who knows but that the darkness is in man?

The doors of Night may be the gates of Light;

For wert thou born or blind or deaf, and then

Suddenly heal'd, how would'st thou glory in all

The splendours and the voices of the world!

And we, the poor earth's dying race, and yet

No phantoms, watching from a phantom shore

Await the last and largest sense to make

The phantom walls of this illusion fade,

And show us that the world is wholly fair.

" But vain the tears for darken'd years

As laughter over wine,

And vain the laughter as the tears,

O brother, mine or thine,

For all that laugh, and all that weep,

And all that breathe are one

Slight ripple on the boundless deep

That moves, and all is gone."

But that one ripple on the boundless deep

Feels that the deep is boundless, and itself

For ever changing form, but evermore

One with the boundless motion of the deep.

" Yet wine and laughter friends ! and set

The lamps alight, and call

For golden music, and forget

The darkness of the pall."

If utter darkness closed the day, my son——

But earth's dark forehead flings athwart the heavens

Her shadow crown'd with stars—and yonder—out

F

To northward—some that never set, but pass

From sight and night to lose themselves in day.

I hate the black negation of the bier,

And wish the dead, as happier than ourselves

And higher, having climb'd one step beyond

Our village miseries, might be borne in white

To burial or to burning, hymn'd from hence

With songs in praise of death, and crown'd with
            flowers !

    "O worms and maggots of to-day
      Without their hope of wings ! "

But louder than thy rhyme the silent Word

Of that world-prophet in the heart of man.

    "Tho' some have gleams or so they say
      Of more than mortal things."

To-day? but what of yesterday? for oft

On me, when boy, there came what then I call'd,

Who knew no books and no philosophies,

In my boy-phrase 'The Passion of the Past.'

The first gray streak of earliest summer-dawn,

The last long stripe of waning crimson gloom,

As if the late and early were but one—

A height, a broken grange, a grove, a flower

Had murmurs 'Lost and gone and lost and gone!'

A breath, a whisper—some divine farewell—

Desolate sweetness—far and far away—

What had he loved, what had he lost, the boy?

I know not and I speak of what has been.

And more, my son! for more than once when I

Sat all alone, revolving in myself

The word that is the symbol of myself,

The mortal limit of the Self was loosed,

And past into the Nameless, as a cloud

Melts into Heaven.   I touch'd my limbs, the limbs

Were strange not mine—and yet no shade of doubt,

But utter clearness, and thro' loss of Self

The gain of such large life as match'd with ours

Were Sun to spark—unshadowable in words,

Themselves but shadows of a shadow-world.

" And idle gleams will come and go,

But still the clouds remain ; "

The clouds themselves are children of the Sun.

" And Night and Shadow rule below

When only Day should reign."

And Day and Night are children of the Sun,

And idle gleams to thee are light to me.

Some say, the Light was father of the Night,

And some, the Night was father of the Light.

No night no day!—I touch thy world again—

No ill no good! such counter-terms, my son,

Are border-races, holding, each its own

By endless war: but night enough is there

In yon dark city: get thee back: and since

The key to that weird casket, which for thee

But holds a skull, is neither thine nor mine,

But in the hand of what is more than man,

Or in man's hand when man is more than man,

Let be thy wail and help thy fellow men,

And make thy gold thy vassal not thy king,

And fling free alms into the beggar's bowl,

And send the day into the darken'd heart;

Nor list for guerdon in the voice of men,

A dying echo from a falling wall;

Nor care—for Hunger hath the Evil eye—

To vex the noon with fiery gems, or fold

Thy presence in the silk of sumptuous looms;

Nor roll thy viands on a luscious tongue,

Nor drown thyself with flies in honied wine;

Nor thou be rageful, like a handled bee,

And lose thy life by usage of thy sting;

Nor harm an adder thro' the lust for harm,

Nor make a snail's horn shrink for wantonness;

And more — think well !   Do - well will follow
        thought,

And in the fatal sequence of this world

An evil thought may soil thy children's blood;

But curb the beast would cast thee in the mire,

And leave the hot swamp of voluptuousness

A cloud between the Nameless and thyself,

And lay thine uphill shoulder to the wheel,

And climb the Mount of Blessing, whence, if thou

Look higher, then—perchance—thou mayest—be-

    yond

A hundred ever-rising mountain lines,

And past the range of Night and Shadow—see

The high-heaven dawn of more than mortal day

Strike on the Mount of Vision!

                  So, farewell.

THE FLIGHT.

I.

ARE you sleeping? have you forgotten? do not
  sleep, my sister dear!
How *can* you sleep? the morning brings the day I
  hate and fear;
The cock has crow'd already once, he crows before
  his time;
Awake! the creeping glimmer steals, the hills are
  white with rime.

II.

Ah, clasp me in your arms, sister, ah, fold me to
  your breast!

Ah, let me weep my fill once more, and cry myself

to rest !

To rest? to rest and wake no more were better rest

for me,

Than to waken every morning to that face I loathe

to see :

III.

I envied your sweet slumber, all night so calm you

lay,

The night was calm, the morn is calm, and like

another day ;

But I could wish yon moaning sea would rise and

burst the shore,

And such a whirlwind blow these woods, as never

blew before.

IV.

For, one by one, the stars went down across the
gleaming pane,

And project after project rose, and all of them were
vain;

The blackthorn-blossom fades and falls and leaves
the bitter sloe,

The hope I catch at vanishes and youth is turn'd
to woe.

V.

Come, speak a little comfort! all night I pray'd
with tears,

And yet no comfort came to me, and now the morn
appears,

When he will tear me from your side, who bought
me for his slave:

This father pays his debt with me, and weds me to
　　my grave.

VI.

What father, this or mine, was he, who, on that
　　summer day
When I had fall'n from off the crag we clamber'd
　　up in play,
Found, fear'd me dead, and groan'd, and took and
　　kiss'd me, and again
He kiss'd me; and I loved him then; he *was* my
　　father then.

VII.

No father now, the tyrant vassal of a tyrant vice!
The Godless Jephtha vows his child . . . to one
　　cast of the dice.

These ancient woods, this Hall at last will go—
  perhaps have gone,

Except his own meek daughter yield her life, heart,
  soul to one—

VIII.

To one who knows I scorn him.   O the formal
  mocking bow,

The cruel smile, the courtly phrase that masks his
  malice now—

But often in the sidelong eyes a gleam of all things
  ill—

It is not Love but Hate that weds a bride against
  her will ;

IX.

Hate, that would pluck from this true breast the
  locket that I wear,

The precious crystal into which I braided Edwin's
 hair !

The love that keeps this heart alive beats on it
 night and day—

One golden curl, his golden gift, before he past
 away.

X.

He left us weeping in the woods; his boat was on
 the sand ;

How slowly down the rocks he went, how loth to
 quit the land !

And all my life was darken'd, as I saw the white
 sail run,

And darken, up that lane of light into the setting
 sun.

XI.

How often have we watch'd the sun fade from us
    thro' the West,

And follow Edwin to those isles, those islands of
    the Blest !

Is *he* not there? would I were there, the friend,
    the bride, the wife,

With him, where summer never dies, with Love,
    the Sun of life !

XII.

O would I were in Edwin's arms—once more—to
    feel his breath

Upon my cheek—on Edwin's ship, with Edwin,
    ev'n in death,

Tho' all about the shuddering wreck the death-
white sea should rave,

Or if lip were laid to lip on the pillows of the wave.

XIII.

Shall I take *him?* I kneel with *him?* I swear and
swear forsworn

To love him most, whom most I loathe, to honour
whom I scorn?

The Fiend would yell, the grave would yawn, my
mother's ghost would rise—

To lie, to lie—in God's own house—the blackest of
all lies!

XIV.

Why—rather than that hand in mine, tho' every
pulse would freeze,

I'd sooner fold an icy corpse dead of some foul
disease :

Wed him? I will not wed him, let them spurn me
from the doors,

And I will wander till I die about the barren
moors.

XV.

The dear, mad bride who stabb'd her bridegroom
on her bridal night—

If mad, then I am mad, but sane, if she were in
the right.

My father's madness makes me mad—but words
are only words !

I am not mad, not yet, not quite—There ! listen
how the birds

XVI.

Begin to warble yonder in the budding orchard
    trees !
The lark has past from earth to Heaven upon the
    morning breeze !
How gladly, were I one of those, how early would
    I wake !
And yet the sorrow that I bear is sorrow for *his*
    sake.

XVII.

They love their mates, to whom they sing ; or else
    their songs, that meet
The morning with such music, would never be so
    sweet !

G

And tho' these fathers will not hear, the blessed

　　　Heavens are just,

And Love is fire, and burns the feet would trample

　　　it to dust.

XVIII.

A door was open'd in the house—who? who? my

　　　father sleeps!

A stealthy foot upon the stair! he—some one—

　　　this way creeps!

If he? yes, he . . . lurks, listens, fears his victim

　　　may have fled—

He! where is some sharp-pointed thing? he comes,

　　　and finds me dead.

XIX.

Not he, not yet! and time to act—but how my

　　　temples burn!

And idle fancies flutter me, I know not where to
    turn;

Speak to me, sister; counsel me; this marriage
    must not be.

You only know the love that makes the world a
    world to me !

XX.

Our gentle mother, had *she* lived—but we were left
    alone :

That other left us to ourselves; he cared not for
    his own;

So all the summer long we roam'd in these wild
    woods of ours,

My Edwin loved to call us then 'His two wild
    woodland flowers.'

XXI.

Wild flowers blowing side by side in God's free
　　light and air,

Wild flowers of the secret woods, when Edwin
　　found us there,

Wild woods in which we roved with him, and heard
　　his passionate vow,

Wild woods in which we rove no more, if we be
　　parted now !

XXII.

You will not leave me thus in grief to wander forth
　　forlorn ;

We never changed a bitter word, not one since we
　　were born ;

Our dying mother join'd our hands; she knew this
    father well;

She bad us love, like souls in Heaven, and now I
    fly from Hell,

XXIII.

And you with me; and we shall light upon some
    lonely shore,

Some lodge within the waste sea-dunes, and hear
    the waters roar,

And see the ships from out the West go dipping
    thro' the foam,

And sunshine on that sail at last which brings our
    Edwin home.

XXIV.

But look, the morning grows apace, and lights the
    old church-tower,

And lights the clock ! the hand points five—O me

　　—it strikes the hour—

I bide no more, I meet my fate, whatever ills betide !

Arise, my own true sister, come forth ! the world

　　is wide.

XXV.

And yet my heart is ill at ease, my eyes are dim

　　with dew,

I seem to see a new-dug grave up yonder by the yew !

If we should never more return, but wander hand

　　in hand

With breaking hearts, without a friend, and in a

　　distant land.

XXVI.

O sweet, they tell me that the world is hard, and

　　harsh of mind,

But can it be so hard, so harsh, as those that should

    be kind?

That matters not: let come what will; at last the

    end is sure,

And every heart that loves with truth is equal to

    endure.

TOMORROW.

I.

HER, that yer Honour was spakin' to? Whin, yer
Honour? last year—

Standin' here be the bridge, when last yer Honour
was here?

An' yer Honour ye gev her the top of the mornin',
'Tomorra' says she.

What did they call her, yer Honour? They call'd
her Molly Magee.

An' yer Honour's the thrue ould blood that always
manes to be kind,

But there's rason in all things, yer Honour, for
Molly was out of her mind.

II.

Shure, an' meself remimbers wan night comin' down
    be the sthrame,

An' it seems to me now like a bit of yisther-day in
    a dhrame—

Here where yer Honour seen her—there was but
    a slip of a moon,

But I hard thim—Molly Magee wid her batchelor,
    Danny O'Roon—

'You've been takin' a dhrop o' the crathur' an'
    Danny says 'Troth, an' I been

Dhrinkin' yer health wid Shamus O'Shea at Katty's
    shebeen ;*

But I must be lavin' ye soon.' 'Ochone are ye
    goin' away?'

'Goin' to cut the Sassenach whate' he says 'over
    the say '—

              * Grog-shop.

'An' whin will ye meet me agin?' an' I hard him
  'Molly asthore,

I'll meet you agin tomorra,' says he, 'be the chapel-
  door.'

'An' whin are ye goin' to lave me?' 'O' Monday
  mornin'' says he;

'An shure thin ye'll meet me tomorra?' 'Tomorra, tomorra, Machree!'

Thin Molly's ould mother, yer Honour, that had
  no likin' for Dan,

Call'd from her cabin an' tould her to come away
  from the man,

An' Molly Magee kem flyin' acrass me, as light as
  a lark,

An' Dan stood there for a minute, an' thin wint
  into the dark.

But wirrah! the storm that night—the tundher, an'
  rain that fell,

An' the sthrames runnin' down at the back o' the
glin 'ud 'a dhrownded Hell.

III.

But airth was at pace nixt mornin', an' Hiven in
its glory smiled,

As the Holy Mother o' Glory that smiles at her
sleepin' child—

Ethen—she stept an the chapel-green, an' she
turn'd herself roun'

Wid a diamond dhrop in her eye, for Danny was
not to be foun',

An' many's the time that I watch'd her at mass
lettin' down the tear,

For the Divil a Danny was there, yer Honour, for
forty year.

IV.

Och, Molly Magee, wid the red o' the rose an' the
white o' the May,

An' yer hair as black as the night, an' yer eyes as
bright as the day !

Achora, yer laste little whishper was sweet as the
lilt of a bird !

Acushla, ye set me heart batin' to music wid ivery
word !

An' sorra the Queen wid her sceptre in sich an
illigant han',

An' the fall of yer foot in the dance was as light as
snow an the lan',

An' the sun kem out of a cloud whiniver ye walkt
in the shtreet,

An' Shamus O'Shea was yer shadda, an' laid himself undher yer feet,

An' I loved ye meself wid a heart and a half, me
darlin', and he

'Ud 'a shot his own sowl dead for a kiss of ye,
Molly Magee.

v.

But shure we wor betther frinds whin I crack'd his
skull for her sake,

An' he ped me back wid the best he could give at
ould Donovan's wake—

For the boys wor about her agin whin Dan didn't
come to the fore,

An' Shamus along wid the rest, but she put thim all
to the door.

An', afther, I thried her meself av the bird 'ud come
to me call,

But Molly, begorrah, 'ud listhen to naither at all,
at all.

VI

An' her nabours an' frinds 'ud consowl an' condowl
wid her, airly and late,

'Your Danny,' they says, 'niver crasst over say to
the Sassenach whate ;

He's gone to the States, aroon, an' he's married
another wife,

An' ye'll niver set eyes an the face of the thraithur
agin in life !

An' to dhrame of a married man, death alive, is a
mortial sin.'

But Molly says 'I'd his hand-promise, an' shure
he'll meet me agin.'

VII.

An' afther her paärints had inter'd glory, an' both
in wan day,

She began to spake to herself, the crathur, an whishper, an' say

'Tomorra, Tomorra!' an' Father Molowny he tuk her in han',

'Molly, you're manin',' he says, 'me dear, av I undherstan',

That ye'll meet your paärints agin an' yer Danny O'Roon afore God

Wid his blessed Marthyrs an' Saints;' an' she gev him a frindly nod,

'Tomorra, Tomorra,' she says, an' she didn't intind to desave,

But her wits wor dead, an' her hair was as white as the snow an a grave.

VIII.

Arrah now, here last month they wor diggin' the bog, an' they foun'

Dhrownded in black bog-wather a corp lyin' undher

groun'.

IX.

Yer Honour's own agint, he says to me wanst, at

Katty's shebeen,

' The Divil take all the black lan', for a blessin' 'ud

come wid the green !'

An' where 'ud the poor man, thin, cut his bit o'

turf for the fire ?

But och ! bad scran to the bogs whin they swallies

the man intire !

An' sorra the bog that's in Hiven wid all the light

an' the glow,

An' there's hate enough, shure, widout *thim* in the

Divil's kitchen below.

X.

Thim ould blind nagers in Agypt, I hard his Riverence say,

Could keep their haithen kings in the flesh for the
Jidgemint day,

An', faix, be the piper o' Moses, they kep the cat
an' the dog,

But it 'ud 'a been aisier work av they lived be an
Irish bog.

XI.

How-an-iver they laid this body they foun' an the
grass

Be the chapel-door, an' the people 'ud see it that
wint into mass—

But a frish gineration had riz, an' most of the ould
was few,

H

An' I didn't know him meself, an' nōne of the
parish knew.

XII.

But Molly kem limpin' up wid her stick, she was
lamed iv a knee,

Thin a slip of a gossoon call'd, 'Div ye know him,
Molly Magee?'

An' she stood up strait as the Queen of the world—
she lifted her head—

'He said he would meet me tomorra!' an' dhropt
down dead an the dead.

XIII.

Och, Molly, we thought, machree, ye would start
back agin into life,

Whin we laid yez, aich be aich, at yer wake like
husban' an' wife.

Sorra the dhry eye thin but was wet for the frinds
that was gone !

Sorra the silent throat but we hard it cryin' 'Ochone!'

An' Shamus O'Shea that has now ten childer,
hansome an' tall,

Him an' his childer wor keenin' as if he had lost
thim all.

XIV.

Thin his Riverence buried thim both in wan grave
be the dead boor-tree,*

The young man Danny O'Roon wid his ould
woman, Molly Magee.

XV.

May all the flowers o' Jeroosilim blossom an' spring
from the grass,

Imbrashin' an' kissin' aich other—as ye did—over
yer Crass !

* Elder-tree.

An' the lark fly out o' the flowers wid his song to
the Sun an' the Moon,

An' tell thim in Hiven about Molly Magee an' her
Danny O'Roon,

Till Holy St. Pether gets up wid his kays an' opens
the gate !

An' shure, be the Crass, that's betther nor cuttin'
the Sassenach whate

To be there wid the Blessed Mother, an' Saints an'
Marthyrs galore,

An' singin' yer 'Aves' an' 'Pathers' for iver an'
ivermore.

XVI.

An' now that I tould yer Honour whativer I hard
an' seen,

Yer Honour 'ill give me a thrifle to dhrink yer
health in potheen.

THE SPINSTER'S SWEET-ARTS.

I.

Milk for my sweet-arts, Bess! fur it mun be the time about now

When Molly cooms in fro' the far-end close wi' her paäils fro' the cow.

Eh! tha be new to the plaäce—thou'rt gaäpin'—doesn't tha see

I calls 'em arter the fellers·es once was sweet upo' me?

II.

Naäy to be sewer it be past 'er time. What maäkes 'er sa laäte?

Goä to the laäne at the back, an' looök thruf Maddison's gaäte!

III.

Sweet-arts! Molly belike may 'a lighted to-night
upo' one.

Sweet-arts! thanks to the Lord that I niver not
listen'd to noän !

So I sits i' my oän armchair wi' my oän kettle
theere o' the hob,

An' Tommy the fust, an' Tommy the second, an'
Steevie an' Rob.

IV.

Rob, coom oop 'ere o' my knee. Thou sees that
i' spite o' the men

I 'a kep' thruf thick an' thin my two 'oonderd a-
year to mysen ;

Yis! thaw tha call'd me es pretty es ony lass i'
the Shere,

An' thou be es pretty a Tabby, but Robby I seed
thruf ya theere.

V.

Feyther 'ud saäy I wur ugly as sin, an' I beänt not
vaäin,

But I niver wur downright hugly, thaw soom 'ud
'a thowt ma plaäin,

An' I wasn't sa plaäin i' pink ribbons, ye said I
wur pretty i' pinks,

An' I liked to 'ear it I did, but I beänt sich a fool
as ye thinks ;

Ye was stroäkin ma down wi' the 'air, as I be a-
stroäkin o' you,

But whiniver I looök'd i' the glass I wur sewer that
it couldn't be true ;

Niver wur pretty, not I, but ye knaw'd it wur
pleasant to 'ear,

Thaw it warn't not me es wur pretty, but my two
'oonderd a-year.

VI.

D'ya mind the murnin' when we was a-walkin'
  togither, an' stood
By the claäy'd-oop pond, that the foälk be sa scared
  at, i' Gigglesby wood,
Wheer the poor wench drowndid hersen, black
  Sal, es 'ed been disgraäced?
An' I feel'd thy arm es I stood wur a-creeäpin
  about my waäist;
An' me es wur allus afear'd of a man's gittin' ower
  fond,
I sidled awaäy an' awaäy till I plumpt foot fust i'
  the pond;
And, Robby, I niver 'a liked tha sa well, as I did
  that daäy,
Fur tha joompt in thysen, an' tha hoickt my feet
  wi' a flop fro' the claäy.

Ay, stick oop thy back, an' set oop thy taäil, tha
 may gie ma a kiss,

Fur I walk'd wi' tha all the way hoam an' wur niver
 sa nigh saäyin' Yis.

But wa boäth was i' sich a clat we was shaämed
 to cross Gigglesby Greeän,

Fur a cat may looök at a king thou knaws but the
 cat mun be cleän.

Sa we boäth on us kep out o' sight o' the winders
 o' Gigglesby Hinn—

Naäy, but the claws o' tha! quiet! they pricks
 cleän thruf to the skin—

An' wa boäth slinkt 'oäm by the brokken shed i'
 the laäne at the back,

Wheer the poodle runn'd at tha' once, an' thou
 runn'd oop o' the thack;

An' tha squeedg'd my 'and i' the shed, fur theere
 we was forced to 'ide,

Fur I seed that Steevie wur coomin', and one o'
    the Tommies beside.

VII.

Theere now, what art'a mewin at, Steevie? for owt
    I can tell—
Robby wur fust to be sewer, or I mowt 'a liked tha
    as well.

VIII.

But, Robby, I thowt o' tha all the while I wur
    chaängin' my gown,
An' I thowt shall I chaänge my staäte? but, O
    Lord, upo' coomin' down—
My bran-new carpet es fresh es a midder o' flowers
    i' Maäy—
Why 'edn't tha wiped thy shoes? it wur clatted all
    ower wi' claäy.

An' I could 'a cried ammost, fur I seed that it
  couldn't be,

An' Robby I gied tha a raätin that sattled thy
  coortin o' me.

An' Molly an' me was agreed, as we was a-cleänin'
  the floor,

That a man be a durty thing an' a trouble an'
  plague wi' indoor.

But I rued it arter a bit, fur I stuck to tha more
  na the rest,

But I couldn't 'a lived wi' a man an' I knaws it
  be all fur the best.

IX.

Naäy—let ma stroäk tha down till I maäkes tha as
  smooth as silk,

But if I 'ed married tha, Robby, thou'd not 'a been
  worth thy milk,

Thou'd niver 'a cotch'd ony mice but 'a left me the
  work to do,

And 'a taäen to the bottle beside, so es all that I
  'ears be true ;

But I loovs tha to maäke thysen 'appy, an' soa
  purr awaäy, my dear,

Thou 'ed wellnigh purr'd ma awaäy fro' my oän
  two 'oonderd a-year.

X.

Sweärin agean, you Toms, as ye used to do twelve
  years sin' !

Ye niver 'eärd Steevie sweär 'cep' it wur at a dog
  coomin' in.

An' boath o' ye mun be fools to be hallus a-shawin'
  your claws,

Fur I niver cared nothink for neither—an' one o'
  ye deäd ye knaws !

Coom giv hoäver then, weant ye? I warrant ye
   soom fine daäy—

Theere, lig down—I shall hev to gie one or tother
   awaäy.

Can't ye taäke pattern by Steevie? ye shant hev a
   drop fro' the paäil.

Steevie be right good manners bang thruf to the
   tip o' the taäil.

XI.

Robby, git down wi'tha, wilt tha? let Steevie coom
   oop o' my knee.

Steevie, my lad, thou 'ed very nigh been the Steevie
   fur me !

Robby wur fust to be sewer, 'e wur burn an' bred
   i' the 'ouse,

But thou be es 'ansom a tabby as iver patted a
   mouse.

XII.

An' I beänt not vaäin, but I knaws I 'ed led tha a
quieter life

Nor her wi' the hepitaph yonder !   " A faäithful an'
loovin' wife ! "

An' 'cos o' thy farm by the beck, an' thy windmill
oop o' the croft,

Tha thowt tha would marry ma, did tha ? but that
wur a bit ower soft,

Thaw thou was es soäber as daäy, wi' a niced red
faäce, an' es cleän

Es a shillin' fresh fro' the mint wi' a bran-new 'cäd
o' the Queeän,

An' thy farmin' es cleän es thysen, fur, Steevie, tha
kep' it sa neät

That I niver not spied sa much as a poppy along
wi' the wheät,

An' the wool of a thistle a-flyin' an' seeädin' tha

    haäted to see ;

'Twur as bad as a battle-twig* 'ere i' my oän blue

    chaumber to me.

Ay, roob thy whiskers ageän ma, fur I could 'a taäen

    to tha well,

But fur thy bairns, poor Steevie, a bouncin' boy an'

    a gell.

XIII.

An' thou was es fond o' thy bairns es I be mysen

    o' my cats,

But I niver not wish'd fur childer, I hevn't naw

    likin' fur brats;

Pretty anew when ya dresses 'em oop, an' they goäs

    fur a walk,

Or sits wi' their 'ands afoor 'em, an' doesn't not

    'inder the talk ! ·

          * Earwig.

But their bottles o' pap, an' their mucky bibs, an'
    the clats an' the clouts,

An' their mashin' their toys to pieäces an' maäkin'
    ma deäf wi' their shouts,

An' hallus a-joompin' about ma as if they was set
    upo' springs,

An' a haxin' ma hawkard questions, an' saäyin'
    ondecent things,

An' a-callin' ma 'hugly' mayhap to my faäce, or a
    teärin' my gown—

Dear! dear! dear! I mun part them Tommies—
    Steevie git down.

XIV.

Ye be wuss nor the men-tommies, you. I tell'd ya,
    na moor o' that!

Tom, lig theere o' the cushion, an' tother Tom 'ere
    o' the mat.

xv.

Theere! I ha' master'd *them!*   Hed I married the
Tommies—O Lord,

To loove an' obaäy the Tommies! I couldn't 'a
stuck by my word.

To be horder'd about, an' waäked, when Molly 'd
put out the light,

By a man coomin' in wi' a hiccup at ony hour o'
the night!

An' the taäble staäin'd wi' 'is aäle, an' the mud o'
'is boots o' the stairs,

An' the stink o' 'is pipe i' the 'ouse, an' the mark o'
'is 'eäd o' the chairs!

An' noän o' my four sweet-arts 'ud 'a let me 'a
hed my oän waäy,

Sa I likes 'em best wi' taäils when they 'evn't a
word to saäy.

XVI.

An' I sits i' my oän little parlour, an' sarved by my
oän little lass,

Wi' my oän little garden outside, an' my oän bed o'
sparrow-grass,

An' my oän door-poorch wi' the woodbine an'
jessmine a-dressin' it grecän,

An' my oän fine Jackman i' purple a roäbin' the
'ouse like a Queeän.

XVII.

An' the little gells bobs to ma hoffens es I be abroad
i' the laänes,

When I goäs to coomfut the poor es be down wi'
their haäches an' their paäins :

An' a haäf-pot o' jam, or a mossel o' meät when it
beänt too dear,

They maäkes ma a graäter Laädy nor 'er i' the
mansion theer,

Hes 'es hallus to hax of a man how much to spare
or to spend ;

An' a spinster I be an' I will be, if soä pleäse God,
to the hend.

XVIII.

Mew ! mew !—Bess wi' the milk ! what ha maäde
our Molly sa laäte ?

It should 'a been 'ere by seven, an' theere—it be
strikin' height—

' Cushie wur craäzed fur 'er cauf ' well—I 'eärd 'er
a maäkin' 'er moän,

An' I thowt to mysen ' thank God that I hevn't naw
cauf o' my oän.'

Theere !

Set it down !

Now Robby !

You Tommies shall waäit to-night

Till Robby an' Steevie 'es 'ed their lap—an' it

sarves ye right.

BALIN AND BALAN.*

PELLAM the King, who held and lost with Lot

In that first war, and had his realm restored

But render'd tributary, fail'd of late

To send his tribute ; wherefore Arthur call'd

His treasurer, one of many years, and spake,

'Go thou with him and him and bring it to us,

Lest we should set one truer on his throne.

Man's word is God in man.'

His Baron said

'We go but harken : there be two strange knights

Who sit near Camelot at a fountain side,

A mile beneath the forest, challenging

* An introduction to 'Merlin and Vivien.'

And overthrowing every knight who comes.

Wilt thou I undertake them as we pass,

And send them to thee?'

                    Arthur laugh'd upon him.

'Old friend, too old to be so young, depart,

Delay not thou for ought, but let them sit,

Until they find a lustier than themselves.'

  So these departed.   Early, one fair dawn,

The light-wing'd spirit of his youth return'd

On Arthur's heart; he arm'd himself and went,

So coming to the fountain-side beheld

Balin and Balan sitting statuelike,

Brethren, to right and left the spring, that down,

From underneath a plume of lady-fern,

Sang, and the sand danced at the bottom of it.

And on the right of Balin Balin's horse

Was fast beside an alder, on the left

Of Balan Balan's near a poplartree.

'Fair Sirs,' said Arthur, 'wherefore sit ye here?'

Balin and Balan answer'd 'For the sake

Of glory; we be mightier men than all

In Arthur's court; that also have we proved;

For whatsoever knight against us came

Or I or he have easily overthrown.'

'I too,' said Arthur, 'am of Arthur's hall,

But rather proven in his Paynim wars

Than famous jousts; but see, or proven or not,

Whether me likewise ye can overthrow.'

And Arthur lightly smote the brethren down,

And lightly so return'd, and no man knew.

Then Balin rose, and Balan, and beside

The carolling water set themselves again,

And spake no word until the shadow turn'd;

When from the fringe of coppice round them burst

A spangled pursuivant, and crying 'Sirs,

Rise, follow! ye be sent for by the King,'

They follow'd; whom when Arthur seeing ask'd

'Tell me your names; why sat ye by the well?'

Balin the stillness of a minute broke

Saying 'An unmelodious name to thee,

Balin, "the Savage"—that addition thine—

My brother and my better, this man here,   ·

Balan.   I smote upon the naked skull

A thrall of thine in open hall, my hand

Was gauntleted, half slew him; for I heard

He had spoken evil of me; thy just wrath

Sent me a three-years' exile from thine eyes.

I have not lived my life delightsomely:

For I that did that violence to thy thrall,

Had often wrought some fury on myself,

Saving for Balan: those three kingless years

Have past—were wormwood-bitter to me.   King,

Methought that if we sat beside the well,

And hurl'd to ground what knight soever spurr'd

Against us, thou would'st take me gladlier back,

And make, as ten-times worthier to be thine

Than twenty Balins, Balan knight.   I have said.

Not so—not all.   A man of thine to-day

Abash'd us both, and brake my boast.   Thy will?'

Said Arthur 'Thou hast ever spoken truth ;

Thy too fierce manhood would not let thee lie.

Rise, my true knight.   As children learn, be thou

Wiser for falling ! walk with me, and move

To music with thine Order and the King.

Thy chair, a grief to all the brethren, stands

Vacant, but thou retake it, mine again ! '

  Thereafter, when Sir Balin enter'd hall,

The Lost one Found was greeted as in Heaven

With joy that blazed itself in woodland wealth

Of leaf, and gayest garlandage of flowers,

Along the walls and down the board; they sat,

And cup clash'd cup; they drank and some one sang,

Sweet-voiced, a song of welcome, whereupon

Their common shout in chorus, mounting, made

Those banners of twelve battles overhead

Stir, as they stirr'd of old, when Arthur's host

Proclaim'd him Victor, and the day was won.

  Then Balan added to their Order lived

A wealthier life than heretofore with these

And Balin, till their embassage return'd.

  'Sir King' they brought report 'we hardly found,

So bush'd about it is with gloom, the hall

Of him to whom ye sent us, Pellam, once

A Christless foe of thine as ever dash'd

Horse against horse; but seeing that thy realm

Hath prosper'd in the name of Christ, the King

Took, as in rival heat, to holy things;

And finds himself descended from the Saint

Arimathæan Joseph; him who first

Brought the great faith to Britain over seas;

He boasts his life as purer than thine own;

Eats scarce enow to keep his pulse abeat;

Hath push'd aside his faithful wife, nor lets

Or dame or damsel enter at his gates

Lest he should be polluted. This gray King

Show'd us a shrine wherein were wonders—yea—

Rich arks with priceless bones of martyrdom,

Thorns of the crown and shivers of the cross,

And therewithal (for thus he told us) brought

By holy Joseph hither, that same spear

Wherewith the Roman pierced the side of Christ.

He much amazed us; after, when we sought

The tribute, answer'd 'I have quite foregone

All matters of this world : Garlon, mine heir

Of him demand it,' which this Garlon gave

With much ado, railing at thine and thee.

But when we left, in those deep woods we found

A knight of thine spear-stricken from behind,

Dead, whom we buried; more than one of us

Cried out on Garlon, but a woodman there

Reported of some demon in the woods

Was once a man, who driven by evil tongues

From all his fellows, lived alone, and came

To learn black magic, and to hate his kind

With such a hate, that when he died, his soul

Became a Fiend, which, as the man in life

Was wounded by blind tongues he saw not whence,

Strikes from behind.   This woodman show'd the

    cave

From which he sallies, and wherein he dwelt.

We saw the hoof-print of a horse, no more.'

    Then Arthur, 'Let who goes before me, see

He do not fall behind me : foully slain

And villainously ! who will hunt for me

This demon of the woods ?'   Said Balan, ' I ' !

So claim'd the quest and rode away, but first,

Embracing Balin, 'Good, my brother, hear !

Let not thy moods prevail, when I am gone

Who used to lay them ! hold them outer fiends,

Who leap at thee to tear thee ; shake them aside,

Dreams ruling when wit sleeps ! yea, but to dream

That any of these would wrong thee, wrongs thyself.

Witness their flowery welcome.   Bound are they

To speak no evil.   Truly save for fears,

My fears for thee, so rich a fellowship

Would make me wholly blest : thou one of them,

Be one indeed : consider them, and all

Their bearing in their common bond of love,

No more of hatred than in Heaven itself,

No more of jealousy than in Paradise.'

 So Balan warn'd, and went ; Balin remain'd :

Who—for but three brief moons had glanced away

From being knighted till he smote the thrall,

And faded from the presence into years

Of exile—now would strictlier set himself

To learn what Arthur meant by courtesy,

Manhood, and knighthood ; wherefore hover'd
    round

Lancelot, but when he mark'd his high sweet
    smile

In passing, and a transitory word

Make knight or churl or child or damsel seem

From being smiled at happier in themselves—

Sigh'd, as a boy lame-born beneath a height,

That glooms his valley, sighs to see the peak

Sun-flush'd, or touch at night the northern star;

For one from out his village lately climb'd

And brought report of azure lands and fair,

Far seen to left and right; and he himself

Hath hardly scaled with help a hundred feet

Up from the base: so Balin marvelling oft

How far beyond him Lancelot seem'd to move,

Groan'd, and at times would mutter, 'These be gifts,

Born with the blood, not learnable, divine,

Beyond *my* reach.   Well had I foughten—well—

In those fierce wars, struck hard—and had I crown'd

With my slain self the heaps of whom I slew—

So—better!—But this worship of the Queen,

That honour too wherein she holds him—this,

This was the sunshine that hath given the man

A growth, a name that branches o'er the rest,

And strength against all odds, and what the King

So prizes—overprizes—gentleness.

Her likewise would I worship an I might.

I never can be close with her, as he

That brought her hither.   Shall I pray the King

To let me bear some token of his Queen

Whereon to gaze, remembering her—forget

My heats and violences? live afresh?

What, if the Queen disdain'd to grant it ! nay

Being so stately-gentle, would she make

My darkness blackness? and with how sweet grace

She greeted my return !   Bold will I be—

Some goodly cognizance of Guinevere,

In lieu of this rough beast upon my shield,

Langued gules, and tooth'd with grinning savagery.'

　　And Arthur, when Sir Balin sought him, said

'What wilt thou bear?'   Balin was bold, and ask'd

To bear her own crown-royal upon shield,

Whereat she smiled and turn'd her to the King,

Who answer'd 'Thou shalt put the crown to use.

The crown is but the shadow of the King,

And this a shadow's shadow, let him have it,

So this will help him of his violences!'

'No shadow' said Sir Balin 'O my Queen,

But light to me! no shadow, O my King

But golden earnest of a gentler life!'

So Balin bare the crown, and all the knights

Approved him, and the Queen, and all the world

Made music, and he felt his being move

In music with his Order, and the King.

The nightingale, full-toned in middle May,

Hath ever and anon a note so thin

It seems another voice in other groves ;

K

Thus, after some quick burst of sudden wrath,

The music in him seem'd to change, and grow

Faint and far-off.

    And once he saw the thrall

His passion half had gauntleted to death,

That causer of his banishment and shame,

Smile at him, as he deem'd, presumptuously :

His arm half rose to strike again, but fell :

The memory of that cognizance on shield

Weighted it down, but in himself he moan'd :

 'Too high this mount of Camelot for me :

These high-set courtesies are not for me.

Shall I not rather prove the worse for these ?

Fierier and stormier from restraining, break

Into some madness ev'n before the Queen ?'

  Thus, as a hearth lit in a mountain home,

And glancing on the window, when the gloom

Of twilight deepens round it, seems a flame

That rages in the woodland far below,

So when his moods were darken'd, court and King

And all the kindly warmth of Arthur's hall

Shadow'd an angry distance : yet he strove

To learn the graces of their Table, fought

Hard with himself, and seem'd at length in peace.

    Then chanced, one morning, that Sir Balin sat

Close-bower'd in that garden nigh the hall.

A walk of roses ran from door to door ;

A walk of lilies crost it to the bower :

And down that range of roses the great Queen

Came with slow steps, the morning on her face;

And all in shadow from the counter door

Sir Lancelot as to meet her, then at once,

As if he saw not, glanced aside, and paced

The long white walk of lilies toward the bower.

Follow'd the Queen; Sir Balin heard her 'Prince,

Art thou so little loyal to thy Queen,

As pass without good morrow to thy Queen?'

To whom Sir Lancelot with his eyes on earth,

'Fain would I still be loyal to the Queen.'

'Yea so' she said 'but so to pass me by—

So loyal scarce is loyal to thyself,

Whom all men rate the king of courtesy.

Let be: ye stand, fair lord, as in a dream.'

　　Then Lancelot with his hand among the flowers

'Yea—for a dream.　Last night methought I saw

That maiden Saint who stands with lily in hand

In yonder shrine.　All round her prest the dark,

And all the light upon her silver face

Flow'd from the spiritual lily that she held.

Lo! these her emblems drew mine eyes—away:

For see, how perfect-pure!　As light a flush

As hardly tints the blossom of the quince

Would mar their charm of stainless maidenhood.'

 'Sweeter to me' she said 'this garden rose

Deep-hued and many-folded! sweeter still

The wild-wood hyacinth and the bloom of May.

Prince, we have ridd'n before among the flowers

In those fair days—not all as cool as these,

Tho' season-earlier.   Art thou sad? or sick?

Our noble King will send thee his own leech—

Sick? or for any matter anger'd at me?'

 Then Lancelot lifted his large eyes; they dwelt

Deep-tranced on hers, and could not fall: her hue

Changed at his gaze: so turning side by side

They past, and Balin started from his bower.

 'Queen? subject? but I see not what I see.

Damsel and lover? hear not what I hear.

My father hath begotten me in his wrath.

I suffer from the things before me, know,

Learn nothing; am not worthy to be knight;

A churl, a clown!' and in him gloom on gloom

Deepen'd: he sharply caught his lance and shield,

Nor stay'd to crave permission of the king,

But, mad for strange adventure, dash'd away.

He took the selfsame track as Balan, saw

The fountain where they sat together, sigh'd

'Was I not better there with him?' and rode

The skyless woods, but under open blue

Came on the hoarhead woodman at a bough

Wearily hewing, 'Churl, thine axe!' he cried,

Descended, and disjointed it at a blow:

To whom the woodman utter'd wonderingly

'Lord, thou couldst lay the Devil of these woods

If arm of flesh could lay him.'   Balin cried

'Him, or the viler devil who plays his part,

To lay that devil would lay the Devil in me.'

'Nay' said the churl, 'our devil is a truth,

I saw the flash of him but yestereven.

And some *do* say that our Sir Garlon too

Hath learn'd black magic, and to ride unseen.

Look to the cave.'   But Balin answer'd him

'Old fabler, these be fancies of the churl,

Look to thy woodcraft,' and so leaving him,

Now with slack rein and careless of himself,

Now with dug spur and raving at himself,

Now with droopt brow down the long glades he rode;

So mark'd not on his right a cavern-chasm

Yawn over darkness, where, nor far within

The whole day died, but, dying, gleam'd on rocks

Roof-pendent, sharp; and others from the floor,

Tusklike, arising, made that mouth of night

Whereout the Demon issued up from Hell.

He mark'd not this, but blind and deaf to all

Save that chain'd rage, which ever yelpt within,

Past eastward from the falling sun.   At once

He felt the hollow-beaten mosses thud

And tremble, and then the shadow of a spear,

Shot from behind him, ran along the ground.

Sideways he started from the path, and saw,

With pointed lance as if to pierce, a shape,

A light of armour by him flash, and pass

And vanish in the woods; and follow'd this,

But all so blind in rage that unawares

He burst his lance against a forest bough,

Dishorsed himself, and rose again, and fled

Far, till the castle of a King, the hall

Of Pellam, lichen-bearded, grayly draped

With streaming grass, appear'd, low-built but

   strong;

The ruinous donjon as a knoll of moss,

The battlement overtopt with ivytods,

A home of bats, in every tower an owl.

Then spake the men of Pellam crying 'Lord,

Why wear ye this crown-royal upon shield?'

Said Balin 'For the fairest and the best

Of ladies living gave me this to bear.'

So stall'd his horse, and strode across the court,

But found the greetings both of knight and King

Faint in the low dark hall of banquet: leaves

Laid their green faces flat against the panes,

Sprays grated, and the canker'd boughs without

Whined in the wood; for all was hush'd within,

Till when at feast Sir Garlon likewise ask'd

'Why wear ye that crown-royal?' Balin said

'The Queen we worship, Lancelot, I, and all,

As fairest, best and purest, granted me

To bear it!'   Such a sound (for Arthur's knights

Were hated strangers in the hall) as makes

The white swan-mother, sitting, when she hears

A strange knee rustle thro' her secret reeds,

Made Garlon, hissing; then he sourly smiled.

'Fairest I grant her: I have seen; but best,

Best, purest? *thou* from Arthur's hall, and yet

So simple! hast thou eyes, or if, are these

So far besotted that they fail to see

This fair wife-worship cloaks a secret shame?

Truly, ye men of Arthur be but babes.'

A goblet on the board by Balin, boss'd

With holy Joseph's legend, on his right

Stood, all of massiest bronze: one side had sea

And ship and sail and angels blowing on it:

And one was rough with pole and scaffoldage

Of that low church he built at Glastonbury.

This Balin graspt, but while in act to hurl,

Thro' memory of that token on the shield

Relax'd his hold : ' I will be gentle ' he thought

' And passing gentle ' caught his hand away,

Then fiercely to Sir Garlon 'eyes have I

That saw to-day the shadow of a spear,

Shot from behind me, run along the ground ;

Eyes too that long have watch'd how Lancelot
    draws

From homage to the best and purest, might,

Name, manhood, and a grace, but scantly thine,

Who, sitting in thine own hall, canst endure

To mouth so huge a foulness—to thy guest,

Me, me of Arthur's Table.   Felon talk !

Let be ! no more ! '

           But not the less by night

The scorn of Garlon, poisoning all his rest,

Stung him in dreams. At length, and dim thro'
    leaves

Blinkt the white morn, sprays grated, and old boughs

Whined in the wood.   He rose, descended, met

The scorner in the castle court, and fain,

For hate and loathing, would have past him by ;

But when Sir Garlon utter'd mocking-wise ;

' What, wear ye still that same crown-scandalous ?'

His countenance blacken'd, and his forehead veins

Bloated, and branch'd ; and tearing out of sheath

The brand, Sir Balin with a fiery ' Ha !

So thou be shadow, here I make thee ghost,'

Hard upon helm smote him, and the blade flew

Splintering in six, and clinkt upon the stones.

Then Garlon, reeling slowly backward, fell,

And Balin by the banneret of his helm

Dragg'd him, and struck, but from the castle a cry

Sounded across the court, and—men-at-arms,

A score with pointed lances, making at him—

He dash'd the pummel at the foremost face,

Beneath a low door dipt, and made his feet

Wings thro' a glimmering gallery, till he mark'd

The portal of King Pellam's chapel wide

And inward to the wall; he stept behind;

Thence in a moment heard them pass like wolves

Howling; but while he stared about the shrine,

In which he scarce could spy the Christ for Saints,

Beheld before a golden altar lie

The longest lance his eyes had ever seen,

Point-painted red; and seizing thereupon

Push'd thro' an open casement down, lean'd on it,

Leapt in a semicircle, and lit on earth;

Then hand at ear, and harkening from what side

The blindfold rummage buried in the walls

Might echo, ran the counter path, and found

His charger, mounted on him and away.

An arrow whizz'd to the right, one to the left,

One overhead; and Pellam's feeble cry

'Stay, stay him! he defileth heavenly things

With earthly uses'—made him quickly dive

Beneath the boughs, and race thro' many a mile

Of dense and open, till his goodly horse,

Arising wearily at a fallen oak,

Stumbled headlong, and cast him face to ground.

   Half-wroth he had not ended, but all glad,

Knightlike, to find his charger yet unlamed,

Sir Balin drew the shield from off his neck,

Stared at the priceless cognizance, and thought

'I have shamed thee so that now thou shamest me,

Thee will I bear no more,' high on a branch

Hung it, and turn'd aside into the woods,

And there in gloom cast himself all along,

Moaning 'My violences, my violences!'

But now the wholesome music of the wood

Was dumb'd by one from out the hall of Mark,

A damsel-errant, warbling, as she rode

The woodland alleys, Vivien, with her Squire.

'The fire of Heaven has kill'd the barren cold,

And kindled all the plain and all the wold.

The new leaf ever pushes off the old.

The fire of Heaven is not the flame of Hell.

Old priest, who mumble worship in your quire—

Old monk and nun, ye scorn the world's desire,

Yet in your frosty cells ye feel the fire!

The fire of Heaven is not the flame of Hell.

The fire of Heaven is on the dusty ways.

The wayside blossoms open to the blaze.

The whole wood-world is one full peal of praise

The fire of Heaven is not the flame of Hell.

The fire of Heaven is lord of all things good,

And starve not thou this fire within thy blood,

But follow Vivien thro' the fiery flood!

The fire of Heaven is not the flame of Hell!'

Then turning to her Squire 'This fire of Heaven,

This old sun-worship, boy, will rise again,

And beat the cross to earth, and break the King

And all his Table.'

Then they reach'd a glade,

Where under one long lane of cloudless air

Before another wood, the royal crown

Sparkled, and swaying upon a restless elm

Drew the vague glance of Vivien, and her Squire;

Amazed were these; 'Lo there' she cried—'a
    crown—

Borne by some high lord-prince of Arthur's hall,

And there a horse! the rider? where is he?

See, yonder lies one dead within the wood.

Not dead; he stirs!—but sleeping. I will speak.

Hail, royal knight, we break on thy sweet rest,

Not, doubtless, all unearn'd by noble deeds.

But bounden art thou, if from Arthur's hall,

To help the weak. Behold, I fly from shame,

A lustful King, who sought to win my love

Thro' evil ways: the knight, with whom I rode,

Hath suffer'd misadventure, and my squire

Hath in him small defence; but thou, Sir Prince,

Wilt surely guide me to the warrior King,

Arthur the blameless, pure as any maid,

To get me shelter for my maidenhood.

I charge thee by that crown upon thy shield,

And by the great Queen's name, arise and hence.'

And Balin rose, 'Thither no more! nor Prince

Nor knight am I, but one that hath defamed

The cognizance she gave me : here I dwell

Savage among the savage woods, here die—

Die : let the wolves' black maws ensepulchre

Their brother beast, whose anger was his lord.

O me, that such a name as Guinevere's,

Which our high Lancelot hath so lifted up,

And been thereby uplifted, should thro' me,

My violence, and my villainy, come to shame.'

 Thereat she suddenly laugh'd and shrill, anon

Sigh'd all as suddenly.   Said Balin to her

' Is this thy courtesy—to mock me, ha ?

Hence, for I will not with thee.'   Again she sigh'd

' Pardon, sweet lord ! we maidens often laugh

When sick at heart, when rather we should weep.

I knew thee wrong'd.   I brake upon thy rest,

And now full loth am I to break thy dream,

But thou art man, and canst abide a truth,

Tho' bitter.   Hither, boy—and mark me well.

Dost thou remember at Caerleon once—

A year ago—nay, then I love thee not—

Ay, thou rememberest well—one summer dawn—

By the great tower—Caerleon upon Usk—

Nay, truly we were hidden : this fair lord,

The flower of all their vestal knighthood, knelt

In amorous homage—knelt—what else ?—O ay

Knelt, and drew down from out his night-black hair

And mumbled that white hand whose ring'd caress

Had wander'd from her own King's golden head,

And lost itself in darkness, till she cried—

I thought the great tower would crash down on
        both—

" Rise, my sweet King, and kiss me on the lips,

Thou art my King." This lad, whose lightest word

Is mere white truth in simple nakedness,

Saw them embrace : he reddens, cannot speak,

So bashful, he ! but all the maiden Saints,

The deathless mother-maidenhood of Heaven

Cry out upon her.   Up then, ride with me !

Talk not of shame ! thou canst not, an thou would'st,

Do these more shame than these have done them-
         selves.'

   She lied with ease ; but horror-stricken he,

Remembering that dark bower at Camelot,

Breathed in a dismal whisper ' It is truth.'

   Sunnily she smiled ' And even in this lone wood

Sweet lord, ye do right well to whisper this.

Fools prate, and perish traitors. Woods have
         tongues,

As walls have ears : but thou shalt go with me,

And we will speak at first exceeding low.

Meet is it the good King be not deceived.

See now, I set thee high on vantage ground,

From whence to watch the time, and eagle-like

Stoop at thy will on Lancelot and the Queen.'

　　She ceased; his evil spirit upon him leapt,

He ground his teeth together, sprang with a yell,

Tore from the branch, and cast on earth, the shield,

Drove his mail'd heel athwart the royal crown,

Stampt all into defacement, hurl'd it from him

Among the forest weeds, and cursed the tale,

The told-of, and the teller.

　　　　　　　　　　That weird yell,

Unearthlier than all shriek of bird or beast,

Thrill'd thro' the woods; and Balan lurking there

(His quest was unaccomplish'd) heard and thought

'The scream of that Wood-devil I came to quell!'

Then nearing 'Lo! he hath slain some brother-knight,

And tramples on the goodly shield to show

His loathing of our Order and the Queen.

My quest, meseems, is here.   Or devil or man

Guard thou thine head.'   Sir Balin spake not word,

But snatch'd a sudden buckler from the Squire,

And vaulted on his horse, and so they crash'd

In onset, and King Pellam's holy spear,

Reputed to be red with sinless blood,

Redden'd at once with sinful, for the point

Across the maiden shield of Balan prick'd

The hauberk to the flesh ; and Balin's horse

Was wearied to the death, and, when they clash'd,

Rolling back upon Balin, crush'd the man

Inward, and either fell, and swoon'd away.

Then to her Squire mutter'd the damsel 'Fools !

This fellow hath wrought some foulness with his

Queen :

Else never had he borne her crown, nor raved

And thus foam'd over at a rival name :

But thou, Sir Chick, that scarce hast broken shell,

Art yet half-yolk, not even come to down—

Who never sawest Caerleon upon Usk—

And yet hast often pleaded for my love—

See what I see, be thou where I have been,

Or else Sir Chick — dismount and loose their
    casques

I fain would know what manner of men they be.'

And when the Squire had loosed them, 'Goodly!—
    look !

They might have cropt the myriad flower of May,

And butt each other here, like brainless bulls,

Dead for one heifer !'

     Then the gentle Squire

'I hold them happy, so they died for love :

And, Vivien, tho' ye beat me like your dog,

I too could die, as now I live, for thee.'

'Live on, Sir Boy,' she cried.   'I better prize

The living dog than the dead lion : away!

I cannot brook to gaze upon the dead.'

Then leapt her palfrey o'er the fallen oak,

And bounding forward 'Leave them to the wolves.'

But when their foreheads felt the cooling air,

Balin first woke, and seeing that true face,

Familiar up from cradle-time, so wan,

Crawl'd slowly with low moans to where he lay,

And on his dying brother cast himself

Dying ; and *he* lifted faint eyes ; he felt

One near him ; all at once they found the world,

Staring wild-wide ; then with a childlike wail,

And drawing down the dim disastrous brow

That o'er him hung, he kiss'd it, moan'd and spake ;

'O Balin, Balin, I that fain had died

To save thy life, have brought thee to thy death.

Why had ye not the shield I knew? and why

Trampled ye thus on that which bare the Crown?'

Then Balin told him brokenly, and in gasps,

All that had chanced, and Balan moan'd again.

'Brother, I dwelt a day in Pellam's hall:

This Garlon mock'd me, but I heeded not.

And one said "Eat in peace! a liar is he,

And hates thee for the tribute!" this good knight

Told me, that twice a wanton damsel came,

And sought for Garlon at the castle-gates,

Whom Pellam drove away with holy heat.

I well believe this damsel, and the one

Who stood beside thee even now, the same.

"She dwells among the woods" he said "and meets

And dallies with him in the Mouth of Hell."

Foul are their lives; foul are their lips; they lied.

Pure as our own true Mother is our Queen.'

'O brother' answer'd Balin 'Woe is me!

My madness all thy life has been thy doom,

Thy curse, and darken'd all thy day; and now

The night has come.   I scarce can see thee now.

Goodnight! for we shall never bid again

Goodmorrow—Dark my doom was here, and dark

It will be there.   I see thee now no more.

I would not mine again should darken thine,

Goodnight, true brother.'

                Balan answer'd low

'Goodnight, true brother here! goodmorrow there!

We two were born together, and we die

Together by one doom:' and while he spoke

Closed his death-drowsing eyes, and slept the sleep

With Balin, either lock'd in either's arm.

PROLOGUE

TO GENERAL HAMLEY.

OUR birches yellowing and from each

    The light leaf falling fast,

While squirrels from our fiery beech

    Were bearing off the mast,

You came, and look'd and loved the view

    Long-known and loved by me,

Green Sussex fading into blue

    With one gray glimpse of sea ;

And, gazing from this height alone,

    We spoke of what had been

Most marvellous in the wars your own

Crimean eyes had seen ;

And now—like old-world inns that take

Some warrior for a sign

That therewithin a guest may make

True cheer with honest wine—

Because you heard the lines I read

Nor utter'd word of blame,

I dare without your leave to head

These rhymings with your name,

Who know you but as one of those

I fain would meet again,

Yet know you, as your England knows

That you and all your men

Were soldiers to her heart's desire,

When, in the vanish'd year,

You saw the league-long rampart-fire

Flare from Tel-el-Kebir

Thro' darkness, and the foe was driven,

And Wolseley overthrew

Arâbi, and the stars in heaven

Paled, and the glory grew.

THE CHARGE OF THE HEAVY BRIGADE

AT BALACLAVA.

OCTOBER 25, 1854.

I.

THE charge of the gallant three hundred, the Heavy
    Brigade!
Down the hill, down the hill, thousands of Russians,
Thousands of horsemen, drew to the valley—and
    stay'd;
For Scarlett and Scarlett's three hundred were rid-
    ing by
When the points of the Russian lances arose in the
    sky;

And he call'd 'Left wheel into line!' and they
    wheel'd and obey'd.

Then he look'd at the host that had halted he knew
    not why,

And he turn'd half round, and he bad his trumpeter
    sound

To the charge, and he rode on ahead, as he waved
    his blade

To the gallant three hundred whose glory will never
    die—

'Follow,' and up the hill, up the hill, up the
    hill,

Follow'd the Heavy Brigade.

II.

The trumpet, the gallop, the charge, and the might
    of the fight!

Thousands of horsemen had gather'd there on the
  height,

With a wing push'd out to the left, and a wing to
  the right,

And who shall escape if they close? but he dash'd
  up alone

Thro' the great gray slope of men,

Sway'd his sabre, and held his own

Like an Englishman there and then;

All in a moment follow'd with force

Three that were next in their fiery course,

Wedged themselves in between horse and horse,

Fought for their lives in the narrow gap they had
  made—

Four amid thousands! and up the hill, up the hill,

Gallopt the gallant three hundred, the Heavy
  Brigade.

III.

Fell like a cannonshot,

Burst like a thunderbolt,

Crash'd like a hurricane,

Broke thro' the mass from below,

Drove thro' the midst of the foe,

Plunged up and down, to and fro,

Rode flashing blow upon blow,

Brave Inniskillens and Greys

Whirling their sabres in circles of light !

And some of us, all in amaze,

Who were held for a while from the fight,

And were only standing at gaze,

When the dark-muffled Russian crowd

Folded its wings from the left and the right,

And roll'd them around like a cloud,—

O mad for the charge and the battle were we,

When our own good redcoats sank from sight,

Like drops of blood in a dark-gray sea,

And we turn'd to each other, whispering, all dismay'd,

'Lost are the gallant three hundred of Scarlett's

    Brigade!'

IV.

'Lost one and all' were the words

Mutter'd in our dismay;

But they rode like Victors and Lords

Thro' the forest of lances and swords

In the heart of the Russian hordes,

They rode, or they stood at bay—

Struck with the sword-hand and slew,

Down with the bridle-hand drew

The foe from the saddle and threw

Underfoot there in the fray—

Ranged like a storm or stood like a rock

In the wave of a stormy day ;

Till suddenly shock upon shock

Stagger'd the mass from without,

Drove it in wild disarray,

For our men gallopt up with a cheer and a shout,

And the foeman surged, and waver'd, and reel'd

Up the hill, up the hill, up the hill, out of the field,

And over the brow and away.

v.

Glory to each and to all, and the charge that they

    made !

Glory to all the three hundred, and all the Brigade !

NOTE.—The 'three hundred' of the 'Heavy Brigade' who made this famous charge were the Scots Greys and the 2nd squadron of Inniskillings ; the remainder of the 'Heavy Brigade' subsequently dashing up to their support.

The 'three' were Scarlett's aide-de-camp, Elliot, and the trumpeter and Shegog the orderly, who had been close behind him.

EPILOGUE.

IRENE.

Not this way will you set your name

A star among the stars.

POET.

What way?

IRENE.

You praise when you should blame

The barbarism of wars.

A juster epoch has begun.

POET.

Yet tho' this cheek be gray,

And that bright hair the modern sun,

Those eyes the blue to-day,

You wrong me, passionate little friend.

I would that wars should cease,

I would the globe from end to end

Might sow and reap in peace,

And some new Spirit o'erbear the old,

Or Trade re-frain the Powers

From war with kindly links of gold,

Or Love with wreaths of flowers.

Slav, Teuton, Kelt, I count them all

My friends and brother souls,

With all the peoples, great and small,

That wheel between the poles.

But since, our mortal shadow, Ill

To waste this earth began—

Perchance from some abuse of Will

In worlds before the man

Involving ours—he needs must fight

   To make true peace his own,

He needs must combat might with might,

   Or Might would rule alone ;

And who loves War for War's own sake

   Is fool, or crazed, or worse ;

But let the patriot-soldier take

   His meed of fame in verse ;

Nay—tho' that realm were in the wrong

   For which her warriors bleed,

It still were right to crown with song

   The warrior's noble deed—

A crown the Singer hopes may last,

   For so the deed endures ;

But Song will vanish in the Vast ;

   And that large phrase of yours

'A Star among the stars,' my dear,

Is girlish talk at best ;

For dare we dally with the sphere

As he did half in jest,

Old Horace ?   'I will strike' said he

'The stars with head sublime,'

But scarce could see, as now we see,

The man in Space and Time,

So drew perchance a happier lot

Than ours, who rhyme to-day.

The fires that arch this dusky dot—

Yon myriad-worlded way—

The vast sun-clusters' gather'd blaze,

World-isles in lonely skies,

Whole heavens within themselves, amaze

Our brief humanities ;

And so does Earth ; for Homer's fame,

Tho' carved in harder stone—

The falling drop will make his name

As mortal as my own.

IRENE.

No !

POET.

Let it live then—ay, till when ?

Earth passes, all is lost

In what they prophesy, our wise men,

Sun-flame or sunless frost,

And deed and song alike are swept

Away, and all in vain

As far as man can see, except

The man himself remain ;

And tho', in this lean age forlorn,

Too many a voice may cry

That man can have no after-morn,

Not yet of these am I.

The man remains, and whatsoe'er

    He wrought of good or brave

Will mould him thro' the cycle-year

    That dawns behind the grave.

————

And here the Singer for his Art

    Not all in vain may plead

'The song that nerves a nation's heart,

    Is in itself a deed.'

TO VIRGIL.

WRITTEN AT THE REQUEST OF THE MANTUANS FOR THE NINETEENTH CENTENARY OF VIRGIL'S DEATH.

I.

ROMAN VIRGIL, thou that singest

    Ilion's lofty temples robed in fire,

Ilion falling, Rome arising,

    wars, and filial faith, and Dido's pyre ;

II.

Landscape-lover, lord of language

    more than he that sang the Works and Days,

All the chosen coin of fancy

    flashing out from many a golden phrase ;

III.

Thou that singest wheat and woodland,

    tilth and vineyard, hive and horse and herd;

All the charm of all the Muses

    often flowering in a lonely word;

IV.

Poet of the happy Tityrus

    piping underneath his beechen bowers;

Poet of the poet-satyr

    whom the laughing shepherd bound with

        flowers;

V.

Chanter of the Pollio, glorying

    in the blissful years again to be,

Summers of the snakeless meadow,

    unlaborious earth and oarless sea;

VI.

Thou that seëst Universal

    Nature moved by Universal Mind;

Thou majestic in thy sadness

    at the doubtful doom of human kind;

VII.

Light among the vanish'd ages;

    star that gildest yet this phantom shore;

Golden branch amid the shadows,

    kings and realms that pass to rise no more;

VIII.

Now thy Forum roars no longer,

    fallen every purple Cæsar's dome—

Tho' thine ocean-roll of rhythm

    sound for ever of Imperial Rome—

IX.

Now the Rome of slaves hath perish'd,

    and the Rome of freemen holds her place,

I, from out the Northern Island

    sunder'd once from all the human race,

X.

I salute thee, Mantovano,

    I that loved thee since my day began,

Wielder of the stateliest measure

    ever moulded by the lips of man.

THE DEAD PROPHET.

182–.

I.

DEAD!

And the Muses cried with a stormy cry

'Send them no more, for evermore.

Let the people die.'

II.

Dead!

'Is it *he* then brought so low?'

And a careless people flock'd from the fields

With a purse to pay for the show.

III.

Dead, who had served his time,

    Was one of the people's kings,

Had labour'd in lifting them out of slime,

    And showing them, souls have wings !

IV.

Dumb on the winter heath he lay.

    His friends had stript him bare,

And roll'd his nakedness everyway

    That all the crowd might stare.

V.

A storm-worn signpost not to be read,

    And a tree with a moulder'd nest

On its barkless bones, stood stark by the dead ;

    And behind him, low in the West,

VI.

With shifting ladders of shadow and light,

And blurr'd in colour and form,

The sun hung over the gates of Night,

And glared at a coming storm.

VII.

Then glided a vulturous Beldam forth,

That on dumb death had thriven ;

They call'd her ' Reverence ' here upon earth,

And ' The Curse of the Prophet ' in Heaven.

VIII.

She knelt—' We worship him '—all but wept—

' So great so noble was he !'

She clear'd her sight, she arose, she swept

The dust of earth from her knee.

IX.

'Great! for he spoke and the people heard,

And his eloquence caught like a flame

From zone to zone of the world, till his Word

Had won him a noble name.

X.

Noble! he sung, and the sweet sound ran

Thro' palace and cottage door,

For he touch'd on the whole sad planet of man,

The kings and the rich and the poor;

XI.

And he sung not alone of an old sun set,

But a sun coming up in his youth!

Great and noble—O yes—but yet—

For man is a lover of Truth,

N

XII.

And bound to follow, wherever she go

Stark-naked, and up or down,

Thro' her high hill-passes of stainless snow,

Or the foulest sewer of the town—

XIII.

Noble and great—O ay—but then,

Tho' a prophet should have his due,

Was he noblier-fashion'd than other men?

Shall we see to it, I and you?

XIV.

For since he would sit on a Prophet's seat,

As a lord of the Human soul,

We needs must scan him from head to feet

Were it but for a wart or a mole?'

XV.

His wife and his child stood by him in tears,

But she—she push'd them aside.

'Tho' a name may last for a thousand years,

Yet a truth is a truth,' she cried.

XVI.

And she that had haunted his pathway still,

Had often truckled and cower'd

When he rose in his wrath, and had yielded her will

To the master, as overpower'd,

XVII.

She tumbled his helpless corpse about.

'Small blemish upon the skin!

But I think we know what is fair without

Is often as foul within.'

XVIII.

She crouch'd, she tore him part from part,

And out of his body she drew

The red 'Blood-eagle'* of liver and heart;

She held them up to the view;

XIX.

She gabbled, as she groped in the dead,

And all the people were pleased;

'See, what a little heart,' she said,

'And the liver is half-diseased!'

XX.

She tore the Prophet after death,

And the people paid her well.

Lightnings flicker'd along the heath;

One shriek'd 'The fires of Hell!'

* Old Viking term for lungs, liver, etc., when torn by the conqueror out of the body of the conquered.

EARLY SPRING.

I.

ONCE more the Heavenly Power

    Makes all things new,

And domes the red-plow'd hills

    With loving blue;

The blackbirds have their wills,

    The throstles too.

II.

Opens a door in Heaven;

    From skies of glass

A Jacob's ladder falls

 On greening grass,

And o'er the mountain-walls

 Young angels pass.

III.

Before them fleets the shower,

 And burst the buds,

And shine the level lands,

 And flash the floods ;

The stars are from their hands

 Flung thro' the woods,

IV.

The woods with living airs

 How softly fann'd,

Light airs from where the deep,

 All down the sand,

Is breathing in his sleep,

    Heard by the land.

v.

O follow, leaping blood,

    The season's lure !

O heart, look down and up

    Serene, secure,

Warm as the crocus cup,

    Like snowdrops, pure !

vi.

Past, Future glimpse and fade

    Thro' some slight spell,

A gleam from yonder vale,

    Some far blue fell,

And sympathies, how frail,

    In sound and smell !

VII.

Till at thy chuckled note,

Thou twinkling bird,

The fairy fancies range,

And, lightly stirr'd,

Ring little bells of change

From word to word.

VIII.

For now the Heavenly Power

Makes all things new,

And thaws the cold, and fills

The flower with dew;

The blackbirds have their wills,

The poets too.

PREFATORY POEM TO MY BROTHER'S SONNETS.

Midnight, June 30, 1879.

1.

MIDNIGHT—in no midsummer tune
The breakers lash the shores :
The cuckoo of a joyless June
Is calling out of doors :

And thou hast vanish'd from thine own
To that which looks like rest,
True brother, only to be known
By those who love thee best.

II.

Midnight—and joyless June gone by,

And from the deluged park

The cuckoo of a worse July

Is calling thro' the dark :

But thou art silent underground,

And o'er thee streams the rain,

True poet, surely to be found

When Truth is found again.

III.

And, now to these unsummer'd skies

The summer bird is still,

Far off a phantom cuckoo cries

From out a phantom hill ;

And thro' this midnight breaks the sun

Of sixty years away,

The light of days when life begun,

The days that seem to-day,

When all my griefs were shared with thee,

As all my hopes were thine—

As all thou wert was one with me,

May all thou art be mine !

'FRATER AVE ATQUE VALE.'

Row us out from Desenzano, to your Sirmione
row !

So they row'd, and there we landed—'O venusta
Sirmio !'

There to me thro' all the groves of olive in the
summer glow,

There beneath the Roman ruin where the purple
flowers grow,

Came that 'Ave atque Vale' of the Poet's hopeless
woe,

Tenderest of Roman poets nineteen-hundred years
ago,

'Frater Ave atque Vale'—as we wander'd to and
fro

Gazing at the Lydian laughter of the Garda Lake
below

Sweet Catullus's all-but-island, olive-silvery Sirmio!

HELEN'S TOWER.*

HELEN'S TOWER, here I stand,

Dominant over sea and land

Son's love built me, and I hold

Mother's love engrav'n in gold.

Love is in and out of time,

I am mortal stone and lime.

Would my granite girth were strong

As either love, to last as long!

I should wear my crown entire

To and thro' the Doomsday fire,

And be found of angel eyes

In earth's recurring Paradise.

* Written at the request of my friend, Lord Dufferin.

EPITAPH ON LORD STRATFORD DE REDCLIFFE.

In Westminster Abbey.

Thou third great Canning, stand among our best

  And noblest, now thy long day's work hath

    ceased,

Here silent in our Minster of the West

  Who wert the voice of England in the East.

EPITAPH ON GENERAL GORDON.

For a Cenotaph.

Warrior of God, man's friend, not laid below,

But somewhere dead far in the waste Soudan,

Thou livest in all hearts, for all men know

This earth has borne no simpler, nobler man.

EPITAPH ON CAXTON.

In St. Margaret's, Westminster.

Fiat Lux (his motto).

Thy prayer was 'Light—more Light—while Time
    shall last !'
Thou sawest a glory growing on the night,
But not the shadows which that light would cast,
Till shadows vanish in the Light of Light.

O

TO THE DUKE OF ARGYLL.

O Patriot Statesman, be thou wise to know

The limits of resistance, and the bounds

Determining concession ; still be bold

Not only to slight praise but suffer scorn ;

And be thy heart a fortress to maintain

The day against the moment, and the year

Against the day ; thy voice, a music heard

Thro' all the yells and counter-yells of feud

And faction, and thy will, a power to make

This ever-changing world of circumstance,

In changing, chime with never-changing Law.

HANDS ALL ROUND.

FIRST pledge our Queen this solemn night,

    Then drink to England, every guest;

That man's the true Cosmopolite

    Who loves his native country best.

May freedom's oak for ever live

    With stronger life from day to day;

That man's the best Conservative

    Who lops the moulder'd branch away.

        Hands all round!

    God the traitor's hope confound!

To this great cause of Freedom drink, my friends,

    And the great name of England, round and

        round.

To all the loyal hearts who long

    To keep our English Empire whole!

To all our noble sons, the strong

    New England of the Southern Pole!

To England under Indian skies,

    To those dark millions of her realm!

To Canada whom we love and prize,

    Whatever statesman hold the helm.

         Hands all round!

God the traitor's hope confound!

To this great name of England drink, my friends,

    And all her glorious empire, round and

    round.

To all our statesmen so they be

True leaders of the land's desire!

To both our Houses, may they see

Beyond the borough and the shire !

We sail'd wherever ship could sail,

    We founded many a mighty state ;

Pray God our greatness may not fail

    Through craven fears of being great.

        Hands all round !

God the traitor's hope confound !

To this great cause of Freedom drink, my friends,

    And the great name of England, round and

        round.

FREEDOM.

I.

O THOU so fair in summers gone,

    While yet thy fresh and virgin soul

Inform'd the pillar'd Parthenon,

    The glittering Capitol;

II.

So fair in southern sunshine bathed,

    But scarce of such majestic mien

As here with forehead vapour-swathed

    In meadows ever green;

III.

For thou—when Athens reign'd and Rome,

    Thy glorious eyes were dimm'd with pain

To mark in many a freeman's home

    The slave, the scourge, the chain ;

IV.

O follower of the Vision, still

    In motion to the distant gleam,

Howe'er blind force and brainless will

    May jar thy golden dream

V.

Of Knowledge fusing class with class,

    Of civic Hate no more to be,

Of Love to leaven all the mass,

    Till every Soul be free ;

VI.

Who yet, like Nature, wouldst not mar

By changes all too fierce and fast

This order of Her Human Star,

This heritage of the past;

VII.

O scorner of the party cry

That wanders from the public good,

Thou—when the nations rear on high

Their idol smear'd with blood,

VIII.

And when they roll their idol down—

Of saner worship sanely proud;

Thou loather of the lawless crown

As of the lawless crowd;

IX.

How long thine ever-growing mind

    Hath still'd the blast and strown the wave,

Tho' some of late would raise a wind

    To sing thee to thy grave,

X.

Men loud against all forms of power—

    Unfurnish'd brows, tempestuous tongues—

Expecting all things in an hour—

    Brass mouths and iron lungs!

TO H.R.H. PRINCESS BEATRICE.

Two Suns of Love make day of human life,

Which else with all its pains, and griefs, and deaths,

Were utter darkness—one, the Sun of dawn

That brightens thro' the Mother's tender eyes,

And warms the child's awakening world—and one

The later-rising Sun of spousal Love,

Which from her household orbit draws the child

To move in other spheres.   The Mother weeps

At that white funeral of the single life,

Her maiden daughter's marriage ; and her tears

Are half of pleasure, half of pain—the child

Is happy—ev'n in leaving *her !* but Thou,

True daughter, whose all-faithful, filial eyes

Have seen the loneliness of earthly thrones,

Wilt neither quit the widow'd Crown, nor let

This later light of Love have risen in vain,

But moving thro' the Mother's home, between

The two that love thee, lead a summer life,

Sway'd by each Love, and swaying to each Love,

Like some conjectured planet in mid heaven

Between two Suns, and drawing down from both

The light and genial warmth of double day.

OLD poets foster'd under friendlier skies,

    Old Virgil who would write ten lines, they say,

    At dawn, and lavish all the golden day

To make them wealthier in his readers' eyes;

And you, old popular Horace, you the wise

    Adviser of the nine-years-ponder'd lay,

    And you, that wear a wreath of sweeter bay,

Catullus, whose dead songster never dies;

If, glancing downward on the kindly sphere

    That once had roll'd you round and round the Sun,

    You see your Art still shrined in human shelves,

You should be jubilant that you flourish'd here

    Before the Love of Letters, overdone,

Had swampt the sacred poets with themselves.

THE END.

www.ingramcontent.com/pod-product-compliance
Lightning Source LLC
Chambersburg PA
CBHW030826270326
41928CB00007B/917